DIGITAL DOWNSIZE

Re-thinking the relationship with the digital world

Nyla Naseer

Published by Temblem Publishing

Copyright © 2020 Nyla Naseer

All rights reserved.

2nd Edition

No part of this publication may be reproduced or transmitted in any form or by any means, electronic or otherwise, without the prior permission of the publisher.

No responsibility for loss occasioned to any person acting or refraining from action as a result of material in this publication can be accepted by the author or publisher..

ISBN-13 978-1-8382422-0-6

This book is dedicated to real friendships

CONTENTS

1	DIGI-TECH SOCIETY	1
2	A FORCE FOR GOOD(ISH)NESS	17
3	IDENTITIES AND HYPER-CONNECTIONS	31
4	A STEP ALONG THE 'ME' CONTINUUM	47
5	FEAR AND FAKERY	57
6	THINKING SKILLS & RESOURCEFULNESS	65
7	REACHING FOR THE TANGIBLE	77
8	COMMUNICATION & INTERACTION	87
9	IMPACT ON WORK	105
10	COMPULSION AND ADDICTION	127
11	DIGI-TECH AND YOUNG PEOPLE	143
12	WISE DECISIONS	153
13	CHANGING YOUR LIFESTYLE	157
14	STEP BY STEP	173
15	ABOUT THE AUTHOR	181

Preface

Digital Downsize is a comment on change and how to manage it wisely. It advocates using technological progress to develop ourselves as people, rather than running the risk of becoming drawn into an unhealthy relationship with the digital world.

Writing Digital Downsize was prompted by observations of people at work, at home and everywhere else that people use technology (so, basically everywhere).

The issues presented in the book have been generated by considering a range of material from blogs to videos, social media applications and websites. I wish to acknowledge the value of all of my sources here, collectively.

The development of this book has been driven by the need to ensure that thought is given to the way that we perceive and use digi-tech, both in terms of mitigating against its ill-considered and obsessive use which has the potential to damage both individuals and society and in terms of its main theme: that technology should be used in a smart, reflective way, enabling rather than disabling the user.

Digital Downsize is an easy to follow introduction to this important and fast-evolving field of thought.

Nyla Naseer

Digi-tech society

The relationship we have with technology has never been so important. As a result of the Covid-19 global pandemic we owe a debt of gratitude to technology for enabling us to maintain contact with others, work from home and look after our health. Covid has made many of us appreciative of the positive input of technology at a time of crisis. Yet we should not lose sight of the full picture; just as digital communications and services have helped us, they also bring with them problems: problems that relate to the power they wield over us and the displacement of our 'human' skills. We also seemingly have few means to rein in the harm that may be caused by their use. As we increasingly see technology as our saviour, we tend to overlook any negatives. Thus, this book is perhaps more relevant now than ever.

The new wave of digitisation that includes online communications, automation, the Internet of Things and a vast range of other technologies such as artificial intelligence and virtual reality, is powering our world and will continue to do so unabated. The digital technology ('digi-tech') referred to in this book is predominantly focused on the internet but other uses of digital technology, such as robotics or surveillance are considered. These also have potentially problematic outcomes, alongside some benefits.

Digi-tech is engendering countless new opportunities for good, from connecting isolated people to information in the UK, to enabling micro-businesses to use payment technology in Africa. Digital Technology is transforming healthcare and other vital services, for example by enabling us to access information more easily and by improving treatments, facilities and training for staff. Online communication is bringing together activists and hobbyists, providing us all with the potential to learn new skills and opening up entertainment like never before. The Internet of Things and Big Data will connect just about everyone with everything super-efficiently, and make everything available digitally everywhere.

5G will bring a new level to connectivity. A truly mind-blowing revolution in the way that we live is happening around us. However, there will be a downside: since the transformation is being led by some of the world's largest digital technology corporations, supported by governments worldwide we might end up losing our civil liberties, privacy and even elements of our basic humanity. It remains to be seen as to whether this is a price worth paying. The erosion of our rights appears innocuous until it means that we are no longer able to make our own choices.

Online information enables people to reach others and become accomplished entrepreneurs, researchers or learners in areas that were, until recently the preserve of the very few. This 'democratising' of information must be juxtaposed against the equally fast growing phenomenon of 'fake' information and, in particular, fake news. Already a growing problem as the world became dominated by identity politics and polarised opinions, the Covid-19 era and global politics has accelerated this phenomenon.

Technology and, specifically, communications technology is on a forward-facing and immutable trajectory. New forms of technology will only become more and more advanced and increasingly integrated into our lives, to the point that our behaviour changes and we can no longer function without them. It could be argued that we are already at this point. The extent to which this happens, and the degree of control that digital technology will assume, depends upon whether we are aware of the implications and, indeed, whether we object. It may be that, given the eagerness with which we have, for example, embraced social media, that we will not only accept but even *demand* this control. As we become used to everything being tailored for us, from suggestions for friends, to what we might like to buy; as we speak to Alexa more than to many of our human friends; as we expect everything instantly to appear once we have ordered it, we will most likely become increasingly comfortable with the idea that we don't mind if omnipotent, generous powers take control or own our personal information. Or we might simply not care.

Most of our fears vis-a-vis digi-tech are not about relinquishing power, but relate to the spectre of things not working: what if my phone is lost or runs out of battery? What if my Facebook account is hacked? What if I can't get online because a server is down? We *want* to be part of the world that matters—and that means online and connected. Our biggest fear is to be disconnected.

For some time, there has been a stirring and murmuring sentiment of concern about the power of some aspects of digital technology—not just in terms of its awesome capacity to do so much, so quickly and so well—but in terms of its potential to take away our individuality and homogenise our thinking, whilst also diminishing some of our most precious skills. This concern may have originally been expressed by people who could not themselves engage with the technology itself, people who had spent decades working without mobiles, computers and, social media. Quite reasonably, given the inability to fully assess the effect of digi-tech without being active participants, these dissenters were treated as Luddites and people who shunned progress. Yet there is now a second wave of concern; a wave that is made up of people who *do* use digi-tech on a daily basis and have done for all of their lives. These people are not scared of using technology or unable to get to grips with new-fangled ways. They are people who, conversely, have been eager to adopt and benefit from digi-tech and its opportunities. They are people well qualified to comment, objectively and in an informed way, on digi-tech and its darker side.

Some of us have started to wake up to the assessment that digi-tech or, more specifically, the way that it is used, is evolving into a monster. We have the sense that we are being swept along by something that is not entirely within our control and is not living up to what we hoped for. Where we had imagined a world of wonderful deep relationships, bringing us closer to new people and experiences, we find instead a world of follow requests from obscure and shady businesses hoping to get us to buy their stuff and constant streams of updates from people who we don't actually know but feel some vague connection with, and hold out a bit of gratitude to for validating our existence.

Where we had a vision of an enriched social life with new forms of entertainment to complement our offline lives, we find that we desperately wait in online queues for latest releases of games that we'll spend several hours a day hunched over a computer to play. Where we had imagined the broadening of our minds by accessing the huge amount of information being added to by the micro-second we find instead that our communicative abilities no longer have to stretch further than adding a link to something, or summarising our thoughts in 280 characters in Twitter's case. Worryingly, our messages are shrinking with time: when Twitter only allowed 140 characters per tweet the most common tweet-length was 34 characters. When the limit changed to 280 characters, the most common length of a tweet dropped to 33 characters. Historically, only 9% of tweets hit Twitter's 140-character limit, with the limit at 280 characters it dropped to 1%.[1] It seems that even with encouragement, we are saying less.

Whatever we are doing, we no longer need to produce something original: we can simply rehash it from something that was rehashed from a couple of other things, which were, themselves copied from somewhere else. Why think originally, when you can just search for a pre-packed solution?

This book is written for people who may just be starting to question what they see around them. Some people may remember a time when people walked down the road without talking into a phone at all, let alone going through a list of

---

[1] https://techcrunch.com/2018/10/30/twitters-doubling-of-character-count-from-140-to-280-had-little-impact-on-length-of-tweets

updates to different social media accounts. People may recall a time when people actually wrote using long-hand, on real paper. I'm not suggesting that this is a preferable state of affairs; but have you ever felt how much your brain seems to connect differently, with your emotions when you actually glide a pen over paper? For those readers I hope that I strike a chord.

But this book also speaks to those people who have never known a time before digi-tech and would find it incongruous (as I would now) to see a scene without a great deal of visible digital communication in it. More to the point, they would find it hard not to engage in anything without the involvement of, or subsequent transfer to, their digi-tech life. Despite the lack of any other frame of reference, it is interesting that growing numbers of these digital natives *are* feeling that something is wrong with the way that things are developing.

Increasing numbers of people are not feeling that they are living 'the dream' that digi-tech was offering to them; a dream with the promise of better relationships, enhanced creativity, information and generally an awesome life. Instead, there are the growing and parallel problems of tech stress and digital addition. That's without even mentioning the wider societal problems of 'dumbing-down' or de-skilling and the issue of digi-tech (especially social media) actually bearing responsibility for intrinsically changing what we want and expect from life.

Our aspirations and interests are increasingly likely to centre on what we feel we and others in society are 'entitled' to, as determined by social media opinion. This is likely to conflict with the views held by other people. For example, social media has fuelled the belief that we should have a world without borders and an equally fervent and opposing belief that we should retain strong borders: feeling entitled does not equate to truly being entitled and the repercussions can be deeply damaging and divisive. The nature of social media means that most people adopt the trending messages of their 'tribe' rather than hold the personal opinions that used to make us the individuals that we are.

Some people are beginning to wake up the nagging feeling that there might be more out there, even if they can't put their finger on it. I sense an element of discontent which I interpret as a 'gut feeling' that there must be more to life than this. Could it be that the sense of discomfort that we feel is because things are becoming just *too* easy? Human life is about challenge, that's what has driven our great histories worldwide. Human beings and real relationships take work; by having much of the 'hard work' taken away from us we also lose the control and challenge that we need to have a satisfying life. Having things easy does not always make us that happy.

To cover technology in general would be impossible since the term encompasses such a diverse range of functions from cybernetics to solar-power. It is the impact of digital communications and applications on the way that we think and behave that is of most concern to this book. Digital Downsize is an intentionally short book.

The book is not meant to be an absolute condemnation of digital technology or communication. To reinforce this point the first chapter highlights some of the many ways that it has and is transforming lives for the better, saving lives and enabling a degree of social and global equality. Who could argue that online training with world-leading experts does not benefit doctors throughout the world? Who could deny that access to information has helped women to, at the very least, be aware of their rights to a more equal life in areas of the world where they have been traditionally disadvantaged? The internet affords people the opportunity, like never before, to do things for themselves: study, find information, publish, express an opinion, bank, and perform. The tools for creativity, at low cost and with tremendous opportunities for innovation, are available to those who seek them out online. However, despite these hugely significant benefits, there is a dangerously seductive and sinister side to digi-tech, meaning that we need to be energised into using it in a more consciously aware way. We need to choose ways to use it as a tool to enrich our lives, rather than allow it to be a 'Pied Piper' leading us, hypnotised, into oblivion. Because digi-tech influences society as a whole, the impact has the potential to change our shared values, for the worse if we let it; we may be getting close to this point.

Digital Downsize will explore the alarming rise of the global social media 'herd'—people and organisations chaotically looking for something to follow, or solutions to problems that they didn't even realise that they had (the age old marketing trick of creating a problem to sell the solution). It examines how, innocently started, this can snowball out of control, drastically changing the definition of what classes as 'normal'. As we are told what to like and what not to like our experiences are increasingly quantified by mentions, follows, links and the like and we start to validate everything we do using these cues.

This book looks at the way that digi-tech is changing society itself. It asks whether the world that is being created by social media is becoming homogenised in some ways and polarised in others and, if so, whether this is something that we should be worried about. Is the very scale of digi-tech something that we can cope with, or are we increasingly becoming slaves to feeding its constant demands?

These pressures have to be juggled within an already uncertain world. The great financial crash of 2007/08, followed by the recession, ushered in an age of austerity, populated by haves and have-nots. In this environment it became easier to become less questioning, more compliant and more accepting of changes that may, in the long-term, work against us. As we looked for an 'easier life' to heal us, it was easy to be lured by the promise of technology-based solutions, without considering the consequences. The era defining advent of Covid-19 in 2020 meant entrusting technology to maintain or repair almost every aspect of our lives, from education to receiving medical attention, or even just not being alone. Whilst technology is credited with saving us, the repercussions are unknown.

Digi-tech has become a beast that has to keep evolving to survive and we are trapped in a cycle of feeding it, hoping it will transform into an obedient puppy rather than a grotesque monster. As we fear being left behind, our dependency on technology is making us unable to recognise, let alone be content with what we actually need to lead a good life.

It is not just the effect of the herd mentality that causes worry. When you have an app for everything why bother doing things for yourself? Digital Downsize explores the effect of digi-tech on our skills. This ranges from the inability to navigate any more when you can have sat-nav, to the problem of people regurgitating research for academic assignments (or using online 'essay-mills' to do the work for them).

Of course, the ultimate de-skilling issue is that of real human ties and interaction. It is hard to believe that people, increasingly tied to the screen, will fully develop the complex skills and judgement needed for satisfying 'in person' relationships; what then will be the effect upon work, families, friendship and society? Is there anything that we can do about this?

Digi-tech is, like electricity or running water, essential to the way we live now, especially so since Covid has speeded up the move towards online-only access to services and things like digital payments; accelerating the rush into a technology, rather than human-centred world. In particular, what are the repercussions of total immersion in a digitally dominated world for young people: the digital 'natives'

People already suffer marked withdrawal symptoms if forced to live without digital communication such as access to social media or gaming. When the agitation of being without this 'fix', disrupts everyday lives, it becomes an addiction. I'll think about the danger signs of social-media and gaming addition and consider whether anything can be done about this growing problem.

The book itself only skims the surface of this fast-evolving topic. It is not an academic text: I have written it from my own perspective and have included what I have observed, or what people have shared with me. I am a prolific user of digital communications and technology myself. I've used digital technology in the writing of the book and in its dissemination. It is not a political book—I leave it up to you to decide how far politics or economics will play a part in what happens with digi-tech. This book aims to provide a bit of conversational background to this issue. I hope you enjoy it.

A force for good(ish)ness

Digitisation has not occurred in a vacuum but as an integral part of a global shift in the nature of social relations and means of production. Thus, it ranks alongside other features of globalisation such as urbanisation, which exemplify the rapidly changing world.

Digitisation is an element in global 'mega-trends such as sustainability, personalisation and volatility in everything from stock markets to employment. Digital technology can bring many improvements, for example in business efficiency, enabling information access and the sharing of skills and knowledge. It also has many undesirable features, including the potential to exploit, mislead and dumb-down at a societal level. It spawns other problems such as providing constant digital distractions which can become addictive, digital narcissism and the use of information as a weapon. It is these problems that this book will concentrate on, whilst applauding the positive use of technology.

At its best, technology enables human development as well as economic growth. In sometimes highly creative ways, it plays a part in reducing poverty, increasing the standard of living, bolstering educational attainment and improving health. It can contribute to building democratic societies marked by involvement, participation and transparency. The role of communication, for example as a means to extend civil society, or even just to extend social relationships, is especially important to this objective. Online discussion, polling and the use of social media to rapidly organize groups to challenge authority in places where dissent has traditionally been almost impossible, are all features that prospectively extend democracy and freedom of expression.

The use of technology in driving forward improvements in the medical, sustainable energy and environmental fields is truly incredible. These changes will herald a new positive and revolutionary phase of development in these fields. There is no question that this benevolent use of technology should and will be encouraged. The issue is one of balancing the support for technological progress with an awareness of how some aspects of technology, predominantly in terms of communications and culture, can cause problems that we need to understand and deal with.

Technology is driving a transformation of philanthropy via disruptive methods: democratising it through global crowdfunding platforms such as Gofundme, Kickstarter and Justgiving. Using these platforms, it is easy to make a pitch for donations and easy to give, giving small projects exposure and much-needed cash. The basis of crowdfunding is emotion-driven, often impulsive giving, with donors identifying with the cause or product area; this makes it a very personal form of giving. Crowdfunding answers the desire that people have to 'do something to help' with causes that they feel close to, whether an emergency appeal after a disaster, funding a new invention or even supporting activist journalism. Although crowdfunding lacks some checks and balances, meaning that there is the potential for fraud, there is no doubt that this is a great way to link causes with motivated, engaged funders.[2]

In the health field, you can find projects on a global scale

---

[2] Rojc, P. (2016, June 28). *Crowdfunding: Who Donates, and Why?* Inside Philanthropy. https://www.insidephilanthropy.com/crowd-cash/2016/6/28/crowdfunding-who-donates-and-why.html

engaged in developing cures for diseases and projects on a local scale putting control into the hands of patients via 'e-health' and telehealth, including expert patient projects, remote patient monitoring and home-based, computer-assisted rehabilitation. Of course, the race for Covid-19 tests, treatments and vaccines has really shown how vital technology is to healthcare now. Digital technology has contributed to every element of dealing with the pandemic: from the use of artificial intelligence and GPS in planning and tracking, screening and contact-tracing to new means of drug discovery and the use of artificial intelligence in diagnostics.[3] Doctors and researchers now collaborate globally on a scale that was previously impossible. Communications technology has enabled us to be better informed and question different approaches to the Covid crisis through political channels. Of course, it also led to conspiracy theories, confusion, frustration and fear as people disagree about the way forward.

---

[3] Whitelaw, S., Mamas, M. A., Topol, E., & Van Spall, H. G. C. (2020).Applications of digital technology in COVID-19 pandemic planning and response. *The Lancet Digital Health*, *2*(8), e435–e440. https://doi.org/10.1016/s2589-7500(20)30142-4

A force for good(ish)ness

Digital communication is being used worldwide to allow people understand and manage their own health, using self-management and remote reporting, for example. The UK National Health Service and healthcare providers the world over are looking to digi-tech to help people to modify their lifestyles so that they are less likely to develop problems: the preventative approach. So, people can turn to online applications to help them to record exercise or diet, or reach out for mental-health support online. In 2020 the NHS launched the 'Better Health' campaign, a downloadable, app-based programme to practically assist and encourage people to lose weight and eat more healthily. Given that apps now dominate the lives of many people, this is a logical and positive step.

As barriers are broken in clinical awareness, we will all benefit from the use of gene therapy and artificial intelligence in health-care. Clinicians (using information collected by apps) will know our risk factors and design treatments specifically for us: the personalised health care approach.

Despite these positives, concern is growing about the wider

lifestyle and wellbeing implications of moving our activities online. We all know that exercise is important; a life glued to screens is likely to make us unhealthy. Strategists have yet to develop effective solutions to humanities slowdown. Physical activity, like mental activity, needs focus; by reducing the mental capacity to do one thing for a reasonable period of time (which physical activity requires in order to make a real impact on health), and pouring scorn on anything that can't be instantly broadcast, digi-tech may be conditioning us out of exercise.

Online-led fitness and connected fitness are still pushing against the tide of sedentary behaviour that, ironically, digi-tech has created. Streamed fitness activities like Peloton and sharing services like MapmyWalk. Fitbit and other fitness trackers have gained an enormous amount of popularity and may now drive exercise in the same way that online dating dominates trying to find a partner. However, although fitness apps are definitely motivating people to become more active, most people still choose inactivity over activity. Digitally-led activity can be expensive, raising questions about fair access. The bare minimum cost of a Peloton bike plus membership for

A force for good(ish)ness

a year is a hefty $2,488 plus tax for the first year.

Ironically, given that many of us are trying to improve our health by using technology, we have simply ended up inactive because it is easier to connect with sport as an online observer.

The immersive role of digital technology in the lives of young people is being researched vigorously, given that they are the first generation born into the internet age. Where digi-tech is used effectively it can inspire young people and bring genuine new learning. However, there is growing concern about the real impact of digital technology on young people's learning, with some feeling that the novelty value may have worn off and that digital technology may not be the panacea that many educators assumed. The six month global experiment in enforced online learning caused by the Covid-19 lockdown acknowledged that although exclusively online learning is an appropriate emergency measure, it may not be sustainable in the long-term. Concerns about a widening of the attainment gap between rich and poor children and the need for young people to develop social skills as they learn, are juxtaposed with an excitement by online educators that the Covid-19 crisis will accelerate the move to mainly online learning, with no going back.

Of course, there is a difference of opinion in the debate about which is best: online or face-to-face learning. Whilst online training may be effective for adults, for young children it may bring many developmental costs. The advantages of online learning centre on its availability and flexibility *not* its quality. In fact used unimaginatively, it can actually drive performance down. There is a balance to be struck and caution is needed before we create a host of potential problems by seeing technology as a panacea for long-standing problems in teaching and learning. Too often assumptions are made about the certainty that things will improve when we 'upgrade' without any real analysis to base this on, or value placed on what has worked in the past.

As we accelerate our rush into adopting more technology as the saviour to our (many) difficult problems in a complex and uncertain world, we can disregard a number of red-flags. The assumption is that we must use the technology because it is there: the first myth that we subscribe to. The second myth is that more technology is better (when a human-centred solution may be best) and the third is that using digi-tech *must* be the answer because people seem to endorse and like it (the emperor's new clothes scenario). These are easy traps to fall into, especially given the whirlwind pace of change.

Many concerns relate to the unimaginative, lowest-common denominator, direction that the online world (in particular social-media) seems to have taken. Undeniably, there is tremendous potential for social media to be used positively and creatively; it's just that more often than not it is used in a trashy way.

The online world may (more or less) create the potential for a level playing field. If you are willing to learn how to do things for yourself the barriers to entry to formerly relatively closed fields such as buying and selling goods and services, stock market trading, broadcasting, writing and music are now open to people. All you need is an internet connection, your products or services and ability to market and deliver them. Online training means that one can learn another language or learn professional skills from the comfort of your own home.

In this way, the internet has created a global community of entrepreneurs, retailers and professionals with a far greater diversity of backgrounds than would otherwise have been possible.

Of course, when barriers to entry are removed many more people enter a market, so competition increases with each new entrant. However, with online tools being available to everybody on more or less the same terms (given a good internet connection anyway) but it is fair to say that it is possible to succeed in new areas which were, until recently the preserve of the privileged few. Hard work and perseverance can be genuinely rewarded online. There will inevitably be disappointment for the many people who don't make it but having the opportunity to try is a big deal.

The internet promotes creativity. You can write anything or share images of anything you create online. You can use YouTube to learn how to do just about anything. Using technology in this way is drawing on its communicative and information functions in an inspiring way and should be commended. Social media can be a very good way of getting messages delivered in imaginative and daring ways. The advertising gurus of the past have been replaced by influencers and paid bloggers. And why not: advertising has a long and creative history after all? Indeed the celebrities off 100 years ago were probably even more sought after for their product endorsements than their contemporary equivalents. Different ways of getting message out are great but it is when it is not clear that we are being sold to that influencer advertising becomes a problem—and when we worship people (and buy products endorsed by them) who have become famous for, well, being famous!

People use their entrepreneurial skills and ingenuity in many ways on the web—not just to make money. Some of the most inventive uses of the web lie in the realms of (benevolent) hacking. Groups such as Anonymous draw attention for their ability to disrupt major corporations and governments, their actions representing technical and creative ability brought together with a socially motivated focus. In addition, these hackers are taking it upon themselves to 'liberate' freedom of expression using technical and creative knowledge. Whilst people might not agree with the objectives, or the methods of 'hacktivists' it is hard to argue against the view that they are, at least, thinking more purposefully than many other social media users.

It may be argued that much of the post-Covid world economy has been preserved by the ability to move activities online. Things like working from home, home shopping coupled with home delivery and remote medical assessments have all meant that parts of the economy and aspects of life that would have disappeared have carried on. Time available as a result of being furloughed has been used for online training and self-development. Covid gifted digital technology its finest hour.

Technology should not become the 'golden-child' to the exclusion of all else, especially in terms of its impact on people in working with it. Technology is a force for good. It has the potential to change our work and lives for the better, enabling us to use our time more productively and enjoyably than ever before and solving many of the problems that have perplexed great thinkers since humanity began. We should not waste this opportunity by simultaneously allowing the way that we use digital technology personally (or in our workplaces) to take away from, rather than add to the quality of our lives.

A force for good(ish)ness

By understanding and thinking about the way that lives are shaped by digi-tech influences such as social media, people and organisations can reflect on the way that they are using it and, if they choose, modify their thinking and actions to ensure that people are the priority. We need to add to the range of our experiences, not allow important activities and skills to disappear. By being conscious not only of the positives of digital technology but also the risks of turning ourselves unquestioningly over to it completely, people ensure that technology works for them, rather than the other way around.

Digital Downsize

Identities and hyper-connections

We live in a virtual environment as well as a 'real' place and our lives are lived increasingly in both. By 2025 there will be nearly 40 billion devices connected to the internet.[4] We already have unlimited capacity online for any quantity of information to be stored and accessed via the 'cloud'. In this environment we have multiple ways to say who we are; we can assume an identity based on our affiliations, interests and habits and connect to others, anywhere, with the same characteristics.

We put our faith in the system, that's human nature. After all the use of digital technology is something about which we appear to have a degree of choice (in terms of how far we participate and how). This makes us feel respected and safe. If, in our 'real' life things are pretty bad, we can turn to the graphically designed and user friendly social media world to escape.

---

[4] https://www.helpnetsecurity.com/2019/05/23/connected-devices-growth/

Our identities now have currency. Our data is there to be mined, bought and sold. Many of us are vaguely aware of this. Most of us don't really care and don't understand what all the fuss is about when people start banging on about civil liberties and privacy. Indeed, if we could sell our own information directly to databases, for hard cash, some people would not hesitate.

As we pour more and more of ourselves into the digital void, we actually provide the *content* for the digital communication machine to work. Historically, this content and information about ourselves would (theoretically anyway) belong to us: no longer. We may contribute willingly because we feel that we are, more often than not, sharing something for the greater good. The digi-tech behemoths—Google, Amazon, Facebook and Apple, for example, all wear their philanthropic hearts on their sleeves and a lot of people genuinely believe that they have an agenda to 'make the world a better place'. Each time the news features a story about some tech giant collecting our personal information to potentially use in some shady manner we give in a little bit more to the inevitability of all of our private information no longer being private.

Identities and hyper-connections

This book is not a comment on any one organisation and its intentions, but it is easy to see that, by laying claim to personal information about what we do online and the content that we produce, companies monetise both our identities and also our content. Services that allow us access to information, or that seem to be doing us a favour (for example by offering us the chance to promote ourselves 'for free') want something in return, and that is information about us to exchange for a slice of the monetary pie. The issue in this case is three-fold: the concentration of power; the presentation of essentially commercial services as social services and the 'creep' of what companies persuade us to give over to them.

We are encouraged to believe that our personal information will be safe by the ever expanding reassurances of tech companies and legislation such as the General Data Protection Regulation (GDPR). However, there is a growing awareness that, regardless of these efforts, anything that one puts online can and most probably will, be accessible to corporations, governments and unscrupulous individuals. Cyber-security is one of the fastest growing industries around, however because of our innate human tendencies: to want people to get to know us, to believe what other people say and to think that really bad things happen to other people rather than to us; security will not prevent our exploitation both by cyber-criminals and by corporations that procure our (unwittingly released) information.

The safest thing to do is not to share too much and thereby avoid losing the grip we have over our own private information. By losing track of personal information we become potential targets for identity theft or even online grooming. By keeping ourselves to ourselves we preserve the dignity of privacy.

Hyper-connectivity allows the real world to connect to the virtual world in ways that can range from the liberating to the frightening. Consider the phenomenon of 'revenge porn' which takes information once considered relatively safe in the 'real world' and throws it online in a devastating, humiliating and hateful way.

Whist living part of our lives online, we have adapted to the risk of too many people knowing the too much by generating different identities: our real-world identities and our filtered on-line identities. This is necessary because we want to protect the 'real' us and also because most people need to live up to the stereotypes that they associate with their online persona, so they create a pseudo-identity that matches the myth. Having different identities and perceptions of ourselves cultivated online will be impactful. Managing different versions of ourselves is not easy, practically or psychologically. Our online personas, even if we try and keep them hidden, might be embarrassing to us or to our employers if they are discovered. Many people regret what they have shared online (perhaps when they were younger) when it eventually catches up with them. Juggling various versions of ourselves may well harm our wellbeing over time.

We live in an 'always-on' world where we have constant access to news and information. This is what we now expect. This always-on situation works to bring us information and entertainment but it also makes its own demands. It demands our attention and our time. We invite information into our personal time seemingly on our own terms but, unfortunately, opening the floodgates means that it is not just browsing the web or social-media that now happens out of hours: work does too. A hyper-connected environment means that work is there for us to access all the time. For some people the opportunity leads to obligation and burnout.

Anything that happens online happens fast—very fast. We want things to happen right now. We need to tell people things right now. We expect success and we don't understand if things don't work out straight away because that is what social media and our hyper-connected lives tell us should happen. When we cannot get results at the speed we expect it causes frustration and panic, even physical illness. The potential for this to affect personal and professional lives is manifestly clear. Since the speed of interaction can only accelerate, it remains to be seen how our lives can be managed so that this is a positive factor, rather than leaving us permanently 'wired'. Maintaining the ability to live life at a speed that affords us the time to reflect and think—to become aware of the elements that give us a quality of life—is a major challenge for the 21st century.

By hyper-connecting us, digi-tech changes and raises our aspirations and we carry our new images of reality around with us, through school and college/university and into the world of work. Our world view is no longer dictated by the people physically around us and that is potentially a very good thing. Someone in a disadvantaged area can be inspired to lift themselves out of their environment by learning about new lifestyles, careers and opportunities. In a hyper-connected world people are no longer necessarily constrained by a lack of knowledge of the opportunities out there. In a re-working of the American dream anyone can become a great lawyer, business person or 'celebrity'. Theoretically, the playing field should be levelled, so that the internet can help people move forward regardless of background; self-accessed information from anywhere can be a substitute for the privilege gained via a posh school or influential family.

However, the potential to access future-friendly, life-affirming and practically useful information is challenged by our conscious or unconscious decision to fall back on less wholesome use of the internet. Although we *can* interact with people with different backgrounds, our natural instincts mean that, more often than not, we tend to stick with people of the same background. Held back by both our insecurities and the capacity of our brains (which, after all, have not expanded exponentially to match the growth of digital communication) we turn to our established networks to tell us what to do. Indeed, once we are in the grip of social media, it becomes increasingly difficult to go against the grain of our group or do something new. We don't even have to make an effort to broaden our network because we have new additions to our 'tribe' suggested for us by the apps to which we have subscribed. In this way we can maintain an illusion of expanding our horizons by adding more people, even if we don't actually know them, or bother to read what they say.

If we do decide to go it alone, away from the security of our extended friendship base, the network can be unforgiving, even cruel. Even if we don't get any actually negative comments, lack of reinforcement can feel just as bad. In our hyper-connected network we need the gratification of people validating us all the time. Not hearing anything is the worst thing possible that could happen, worse even than people speaking against us because in the online world *anything* is better than silence.

We could, of course, switch off and unplug. But, who would we be then? Being disconnected 'invisible' is equivalent to not existing at all. As we devote more and more of our energy (actively and persuasively steered by digi-tech) to creating our virtual lives, our offline lives change in nature; for some essentially providing the material with which to build our hyper-connected selves. Unplugging ourselves from the network becomes untenable; the more people you are linked to the harder it becomes. For increasing numbers of people being bereft of their connected identity would leave them in a position of almost infantile inability to cope with some aspects of life, ranging from finding their way around to knowing what to wear or even what to eat.

For most people this is an extreme scenario, I hope that the ability to manage our lives in the real and simultaneously in the online world is something that will not cause the problems that are hinted at. I suggest that the best course of action is to understand the relationships that exist between people and digi-tech, where these relationships have come from and where they are going. By doing this, individuals and organisations *can* accommodate both of their hyper-connected worlds.

Digi-tech, especially social media, is spearheading the most significant changes to society ever known to mankind. We now live in a world where your value in the real world is increasingly judged by your antics and, especially, your 'popularity' in the virtual world. What is more, we willingly propagate and feed this illusion. Social media is an agent of social change; indeed, this is something that social media companies themselves want us to understand. They devote a great deal of time and money to flaunt their credentials in enabling people to start dynamic activity with a number and diversity of people that would have been totally impossible ten years ago.

We are encouraged to find out what is happening in the lives of others, link with them and change our own lives and, sometimes, the world around us for the better. For some people that is what will happen; for the others it is not. For the vast majority of people, social media, e-leisure, e-working and the like, means being part of a 'matrix' of dependent usernames, drawn into the dopamine-fuelled illusion of our online lives. In a post-Covid world it will be a necessity.

The scale of the issue is not something that I will dwell on, by

Identities and hyper-connections

the time you read this the hundreds of millions of emails, messages, tweets and so on sent per day will already have increased by exponential factors over when the book was written. It is enough to say that the interval between people checking their screens is in the minutes and the numbers of social media accounts is counted in the billions. You don't need a book to tell you how intensively digital communication is used. It is as if any experience is not real until you have broadcast it to the online world. Food-porn sits happily with conspiracy theories, which sit alongside memes and compete for attention with actual events. Anything which we feel is of consequence triggers a frenzy to share and a panic to validate the experience by posting the evidence online. Social experiences, rather than being valued for their own sake, are now mere opportunities to broadcast to followers, fans and friends. Merely being in the moment has become the preserve of hard-core rationalists and mindfulness practitioners.

Hang on a minute, if we spread something around our social-media community, isn't the experience then 'shared'? Well no, not really, sharing is an emotional experience, not a thumbs-up icon on a screen. We now live in a culture of insecurity where we are, increasingly, no longer able to operate without the electronic validation of others. Our value systems are changing. Social media is enabling a world of tense, worried users. This anxiety is about lots of connected issues, all of which seem to sap away at our ability to be independent and resourceful, confident or resilient.

We have reached a point where an entire generation grows up with social media accounts in-situ from school age. The 'digital' birth of some babies in the United States precedes the actual birth by several months. This includes getting domain names, websites and social media accounts before birth.[5] The fight to give your child a head start in life now begins online.

A study by The Office of the Children's Commissioner for England found that when children get their own social media accounts, around age 11, they will post about 70,000 times before they turn 18 and that many children too young to use the internet are also using "internet-connected toys", many of

---

[5] *BBC News Website. February 2013. See::*
 How 'big data' is changing lives: www.bbc.co.uk/news/technology-21535739

which gather personal information and messages.[6] These alarming statistics highlight the pressure on young people to be connected online; if you are not connected you are outside the major frame of reference of your peers. Essentially, the choice is between social media or risking social isolation. The network, with all its associated security risks, *is* the real world for young people.

From the moment that you sign up to your social media account, the pressure for many is on to collect as many followers as possible in order to validate your existence. The early stages of operating a profile, when people try and generate follower traction, can be very stressful. Without followers you are nobody. With followers, not only are you 'somebody' but the lucky ones can make a lot of money, with the top five Instagrammers earning around a cool $1million per post. It is no wonder that young people want to share in the riches that being an influencer can lead to. Sadly, it seems

---

[6]. https://www.childrenscommissioner.gov.uk/2018/11/08/childrens-commissioners-report-calls-on-internet-giants-and-toy-manufacturers-to-be-transparent-about-collection-of-childrens-data/

that having your own influencer channel does nothing for dispelling stereotypes about gender, since the vast majority of women post about 'beauty and lifestyle' whereas men have channels devoted to 'humour', pranks or sport. Nor does it appear to lead to happiness, either for the influencers (who are under constant pressure to maintain their often fake personas) or for followers. Indeed suicide rates are at multi-decade highs for teenagers, with social media being held up as a major cause for depression in this age group. Anxiety and insecurity is potentially built in to each element of social media use, from signing up onwards.

Once you have the hoped for clan, the next element of anxiety is to actually maintain the stream of communication that takes you to the next level of ego stroking; this is where the real problems set in. You cannot control what people might say or do at any point in time. Your only choice is to feed the social media beast with the fodder it likes and that is generally short, devoid of thought, overly dramatic and lacking individuality. You then sit and wait for approval from your network. This need for constant approval is accepted across society and upheld by our major cultural references. If you go onto a news

Identities and hyper-connections

site/blog/event, you are urged to like or share the story, even if you have not read it, are not really sure what it is about and have no real interest in it. Any encounter, no matter how tenuous, provides an opportunity for additional followership.

Once engaged with social media we get used to liking and sharing willy-nilly without discernment. Many will endorse anything, regardless of whether we have any experience of whatever it is we are giving a nod to. Fake reviews and posts, often generated in China or Russia make the picture even more confusing. This cheapens the whole process of reviews, with the irony being that review sites such as Trip Adviser or Trust Pilot and internet giants like Amazon being exposed for allowing fraudulent reviews.[7]

---

[7] https://www.ft.com/content/bb03ba1c-add3-4440-9bf2-2a65566aef4a

Digital Downsize

A step along the 'me' continuum

For a couple of decades now we have been in the grip of an ever expanding obsession with 'celebrity' and (especially young) people's personal association with it. It is not just that people admire and want to emulate the people they see on-screen anymore; social media is playing a part in convincing some people that they actually *have* the qualities that they rate in their celebrity heroes, whether these are looks, intelligence, wit, or other skills—even if these are completely untested or evidenced. It seems that, for an increasing number of young people, telling yourself and other people that you do have those qualities is all that is needed to make it a reality. This creates a very dangerous sense of entitlement and self-delusion.

The iconic American Freshman Survey began in 1966 and has been completed by about nine million young people. This survey gives an insight into how young people compare themselves to their peers according to a number of basic skills.

Since the survey began there has been a dramatic rise in the number of students who describe themselves as being 'above average' for individualistic traits like academic ability, drive to achieve, mathematical ability and self-confidence. Less individualistic traits, such as understanding others and spirituality, when self-appraised saw little change or a decrease over the same period. The study also reveals a disconnect between the student's opinions of themselves and actual ability, with students feeling that they are gifted in areas (such as writing) or 'have a drive to succeed', whereas the facts about their actual ability (derived from test results) and the work they put into succeeding (hours worked) contradict their opinions of themselves.[8]

Professor Jean Twenge of San Diego State University has suggested there has been a 30% tilt towards narcissistic attitudes (vanity; self-admiration, self-centredness) in US students since 1979.[9] These attitudes are not only incredibly

---

[8] *Reported by William Kremer, BBC World Service. January 2013 Does confidence really breed success? See: http://www.bbc.co.uk/news/magazine-20756247*

[9] *Jean Twenge. 2007. Generation Me: Why Today's Young Americans Are More Confident, Assertive, Entitled--And More Miserable Than Ever Before. Free Press.*

infuriating for other people but also likely to result in disappointment with life further down the line when people realise that doors to opportunity, wealth and fame don't just fly open as we walk towards them.

The fact that social media, alongside its close cousin, celebrity culture, actively promotes the cult of entitlement in question and allows people to appear more successful than they actually are, is surely one element in the delusions that some people hold about themselves? It is good to have high self-esteem, but this needs to be based on the outcomes that people have achieved *not* the shallow validations of social media.

Entitlement promoted by social media has been greatly added to by the vast array of belief systems telling people that is they 'want' something enough, it will come to them and that 'positive thought' will reward them regardless of any realistic barriers that people need to personally overcome with effort. We live in the daily 'positive message' world. It is my belief that this unrealistic mindset leads to over-inflated egos, disappointment and even mental health problems. The popularity of 'manifesting your life' videos on TikToks is one of a range of similar ways of sharing the belief that you can create your own reality just by thinking it (and presumably also sharing it online). Having a positive mindset can help people to reach goals, however many 'manifestation' believers are likely to end up disappointed. The idea that believing in yourself will bring any outcome you hope for is simply delusional and yet millions of young people now genuinely think this way.[10]

The appeal of digital technology—the apparent complete control that we have over what we do, who we see, where we go and who we engage with—does not do a lot to develop our thinking skills. Online, relationships are disposable; we can remove people from our network and fill the gap with instant replacements. It seems that we are the masters of our own little universe. Compare this to real life, where we have to contend with confrontation and disappointment every day and where we need to put genuine work into improving ourselves and our lives.

---

[10] https://www.bbc.co.uk/bbcthree/article/6c81cb01-d8f1-46d3-909a-c3493add8c8e

A step along the 'me' continuum

The irony is that in our online lives we have far *less* control that we believe that we do. We are able to build a parallel identity, but the identity itself breaks down under any challenge. What is worse is that our online identities lull us into a false sense of our own abilities, power and importance. It is when we have to exhibit our abilities in the real world that the illusion breaks down.

For some people, young people especially, empathy with experiences that lie outside this connected world is limited. There are horror stories of the behaviour of people filming abuse for broadcast, but we don't need to go as far as this to see the way that our own behaviour is shaped by our online, connected world view. If we are caught up in a natural disaster, crime or unfortunate event and, increasingly, our first reaction is not to reach out and help any more, or even to make ourselves safe: it is to capture the image or inform our network.

We appear to be losing the ability to empathise rationally with the experiences and urgent needs of other people. Priorities have shifted so that, for some, the need to broadcast eclipses, sometimes completely, the need to help or not to harm. In the worst scenarios we stop seeing other people as people at all: rather they become props for our online stories. By becoming more 'connected' to our network we are disconnecting ourselves from everyone else.

It is simply easier to be told what to like and how to tell others about it. In the proliferation of information that we have access to, we need a helpful being to guide us and the social media networks willingly provide this.

Social media is actively setting the agenda for what we should be thinking and aspiring to. But hold on—isn't it *us* who provide the content and therefore set the agenda? The mechanisms of social media: likes, trends, favourites or whatever, *steer* us towards what is important. In this way we collectively understand the expectations of the online community that we are part of and we modify our behaviour to fit in.

The very essence of social media is the importance of 'sharing', whether thoughts, pictures, songs or messages. The more we share these personal items with each other the more

A step along the 'me' continuum

we are likely also to share other information and preferences. Once engaged with social media we get used to sharing. This means we look for experiences to share and there is a whole world of obliging apps ready and waiting to help us with sharing our consumer activities. These apps allow us to automatically send out updates on where we have bought clothes or our leisure activities, for example. This is yet another way of sacrificing our own personal identity and data to commercial organisations.

It seems that many people are particularly keen on sharing pictures of cats or other pets. I guess cats are cute but, with respect, is it reasonable to spend many hours a day looking through pictures of pets, as many people now do?

You can go to any number of sites to find out what is trending; although some keywords are about current affairs and generate debate, many other trends are less worthy and celebrity or product led—or fluffy animals. The 'news' may be real or contrived and 'fake'; it becomes harder and harder to sort fact from fiction.

This is part of a far bigger debate about the media in general, but if the popularity stakes are being led by celebrity gossip and fake news, a natural outcome would appear to be the continued dumbing down and polarisation of society. The best efforts of rationalists aiming to counter this trend cannot hope to compete with the pressures of social media. A cynic would contend that a dumber, more homogeneous profile makes people more easily controlled (within their particular 'echo chamber') and marketing easier.

The carefully crafted images of influencers press people to 'prove' that they are part of the 'family'. Much of the time this is fairly innocuous. However, the trend of disturbing, even bullying 'prank' videos shared by some vloggers, shows the capacity of some influencers to encourage dark and risky behaviour. The more fans they generate, the more likely we are to see and endorse their videos. Given the sometimes breathtakingly foolhardy way that the most extreme prank vloggers behave, with an increasing number dying as a result of their stunts, ever more tragic results will occur.[11] As vlogging becomes a career of choice for more people, so chasing the

---

[11] https://www.fastcompany.com/90287323/people-are-falling-off-buildings-in-search-of-the-perfect-instagram-shot

associated income will demand more and more sensationalist output. Normalising this behaviour is not going to be good for society—the power to control followers can be very dangerous.

In the 'real' world, situations and lives are more complex than the snippets on social media. However, even our offline lives are often not really offline because they are constantly being transmitted online. This means that our experiences, like our discussions, have to be filtered through a prism to make them acceptable for our social media world. Every life event can no longer be a private experience; otherwise we face accusations of 'selfishly' keeping it to ourselves. If we buy, eat or view something, we need to tell others alongside actually doing it. If someone you care about dies, what matters more than anything else is the number of sympathy messages on Facebook or Twitter. The most private occasions *must* be made painfully public for some people to feel that they are being properly acknowledged. The consequences of this strike me as sad and rather sinister.

What do 'share' buttons really do past create the opportunity to bypass telling people in more depth about what we find interesting and useful, replacing this with the convenience of pressing a button? Sharing, apart from being an information gathering, marketing and product pushing exercise by companies, is often just a way of dealing with the insecurity of not being sufficiently engaged and connected to the group you associate yourself with. This yearning for acceptance also makes us susceptible to other dark aspects of the internet, for example fake news and fear mongering.

Fear and fakery

The online world is a breeding ground for fear and misinformation. The very qualities that make online communication and, in particular, social media so attractive: speed, ubiquity and openness to anybody that wants to post on it, mean that it is impossible to filter the honest and true from the doubtful and fake. Given a veneer of authenticity by tailoring the look of a message or article, bizarre theories can become accepted truths, believed and endorsed by millions of people around the world in a matter of days.

Social media exposes people to misleading or downright fake content in the form of hoaxes, rumors, conspiracy theories, fabricated reports and click-bait headlines. The rationale for this tends to be either to make money: typically health or investment related posts, which drive traffic to ads; or political/ideological: typically smear stories about groups of people or events. The repercussions are ominous: from encouraging dangerous beliefs about health, to manipulation of people wanting to invest money, to attempts to skew results of elections. Our human brains make us vulnerable to relatively simple manipulative techniques. The addition of algorithms which bump content up based on engagement, rather than trustworthiness, accelerates the spread and belief in fake, low-quality news.

As our social networks are polarised anyway, we are likely to receive news and information already biased towards our world-view, further convincing us of the veracity of the news. This confirmation-bias then reinforces our ever strengthening belief that we are right and other people, who don't think like us, are wrong. The more fake news we get, the more it confirms itself and the more we think of it as accurate. The truth can then be hard to find.

This would be bad enough if it was just teams of people sending out this fake information. However, 'social bots' controlled by software, also trawl the internet feeding it with lies. Because the bots appear to be 'real' people, interacting with us and appealing to our tendency to believe others 'like us', we buy in to their posts and disseminate them still further.

Fear and fakery

Much fake news fits into the definition of conspiracy theory. In recent years these have been skewed towards spreading fear, either about other people, or about policies such as vaccination. The Covid-19 crisis took fake news to a new level as theories flooded the internet about how the virus started; mismanagement, cures, and vaccines. The fast changing nature of the crisis supplied a perfect backdrop to fake news; providing new 'proof' of unproven or fake theories at each twist and turn.

Another very active area of fake news relates to the need to be vigilant and fearful of people who are not 'like us'. Made up, but plausible sounding stories make out that various groups of people are not to be trusted, or even dangerous. Our natural inclination to distrust and fear other types of people has led to the passionate hatred of those who differ from us, especially people with a different political or religious belief, or indeed, lack of belief.

Conspiracy theories have pre-dated social media of course, debates about who really killed JKF or whether the moon-landing was faked, or who was responsible for the September

11th attacks are part of life. However, the theories spread online take hold in a matter of days rather than years and attract the unquestioning belief of millions within that timeframe.

As a result, many of us are fearful of something or someone; our fears stoked by seemingly plausible social media information. This creates a general atmosphere of suspicion and fear which has repercussions for where we go and how we behave in the offline world. We become more and more entrenched in the bubble of 'people like us' where our emotions can be whipped up by fear, panic or feeling morally superior.

Fake news is only likely to harden opinions on both sides of an ideological divide. Contrary to the people who still feel that minds can be changed, this becomes increasingly unlikely as people become more and more entrenched in their views. Campaigners are literally wasting their time 'preaching to the converted' since there is little room for ideological diversity. Genuine argument becomes the loser.

The resulting bitterness means that some people no longer

feel comfortable with expressing views that are either divergent from their 'identity peers' or question some aspect of trending behaviour. Moral pressure should never, in my view, close down legitimate debate or attempt to humiliate or denigrate people for sharing their opinion or experiences, even if this does not fit the prevailing narrative. Assuming that your group are the 'good guys' and labelling other groups of people as somehow lesser beings deserving of abuse is an extremely retrograde development.

Social media promotes hostility and fear in other ways too. By hosting truly horrific videos of torture, death and inhumanity the online world is a shop window for terror and fear. Generalised fear leaches into the real world where we can be haunted by the spectre of bad things happening closer to home. Of course the images can also be manipulated and presented as part of the fake news agenda.

The fears felt generated by fake information as accompanied by our own, internal fears of not fitting in. We are terrified of being found to be wanting in terms of our allegiance to whatever cause our tribe is aligned with, be this political or social. Therefore the insecurities built in to social media reinforce each other in a doubly destructive way.

What is apparent is that the online world, with its potential to ignite division and fear, has deeply affected how we behave in the real world. No longer carefree, we now gravitate towards 'bubbles' of 'safe' people and view outsiders with suspicion. A subtle change has occurred over time whereby an atmosphere of uncertainty intrudes into many areas of life, leaving people feeling unable enjoy life with the same freedom as in the past. We no longer walk alone at night for fear of running into the wrong people, we retreat to our own neighbourhoods instead of exploring and debates are a no-go due to a fear of being confronted by people we don't like and don't want to listen to.

In the next section, I'm going to explain that, not only does an imbalanced relationship between people and digital technology take away our control over our lives, but also that it is actually changing society (and us) in another related way: de-skilling. By handing over our tasks to the tech machine we sign over our abilities, sometimes in the most basic of ways and with the most basic of skills—human interaction itself. I look at how this is achieved what sort of difference this could

Fear and fakery

make to our lives.

Digital Downsize

Thinking skills and resourcefulness

The concern of this book is the balance between people and digi-tech and the preservation of a relationship in which digi-tech communication is a tool that enhances our lives rather than detracting from our quality of life, or (worse) harming us. With any kind of technological or social change it is very hard to wind things back, or undo damage. For this reason, I want to discuss the impact of digi-tech on skills.

Although technology will lead to a major destruction of jobs over the next couple of decades, in this book I'm not really going to discuss the loss of jobs as technology replaces people. In fact, for some industries it could be seen as a good thing that technology has taken over: making things safer, taking over the very routine and boring and allowing people theoretically to concentrate on higher level activities. Neither would I deny that technology enhances many areas of work, especially the outcomes of professions such as engineering or surgery. Robotics and simulation have and will continue to benefit the skills and expertise of people and inspire many others. Alongside these positive developments however, some fundamental skills will be changed and, potentially, damaged. The skills that I am referring to relate predominantly to communications oriented digi-tech and may be summarised as:

- Thinking and resourcefulness and
- Communication, interaction and social skills

These skills start to be shaped as soon as we are born and are influenced heavily by our experiences as young people. However, the skills of all of us, no matter what our age, are affected as a consequence of us being part of a wider society.

Our lives are now hyper-connected: encompassing our offline 'real' space as well as our online virtual space. This has massive implications for the skills that we need. To succeed in the modern world, we need to enhance our skill set. We need real world skills, as well as virtual world skills. Digital skills are increasingly absorbed by us from an early age and become second (or first?) nature. However, the impact of gaining and operating with these skills may not sit easily with the skill set

Thinking skills and resourcefulness

that we need for our 'real' lives and the result may be a reduced ability to perform effectively in the real world. Even worse, being brought up on a diet of digi-tech may modify the skill set of an entire society if we are not careful.

Digi-tech communications lend themselves to being short, sweet and fairly immediate. Texts and tweets are measured in characters and social media messages are short and snappy. Emojis and status updates don't really extend the writing and communicative skills of most people. Immediacy has replaced depth in the online communications: we are often less concerned by the content as the speed of the communication that we receive—we need a quick reply. We attribute thought and depth to someone pressing a 'like' button and value its immediate feedback.

People rely on the first plausible looking bit of information that they find, rather than researching anything to gain a rounded perspective. Both facts and opinions are presented online in the same way by search engines and many people readily accept the veracity and validity of both as equal. The repercussions of this are sinister in my opinion, allowing made-up news to spread like wild-fire across the web. The popularity of conspiracy theories and fake news is testament to how easy it is to have people believe what is written online. 'QAnon' is the latest and most legitimised and influential group which, by popular opinion, is based largely on fake news.

The cut and paste generation is here to stay. Colleges and universities are fighting an almost impossible battle to stop the twin track problems of direct plagiarism and the readily available online services of essay writers. One in seven students globally are thought to be cheating, either in exams or through the use of online essay mills—contract cheating.[12] The quality of the bought essays is diminishing, as the pool of people able to write originally shrinks and the pool of writers willing to try to rehash available information increases. Diminishing quality is likely to be contributing to 'grade inflation' in British universities and elsewhere. The most worrying aspect of this epidemic-sized problem is that the professionals of the future are leaving universities not with genuine skills and knowledge but with credentials that are fraudulent. Would you want to be treated by a fake doctor or

---

[12] https://www.frontiersin.org/articles/10.3389/feduc.2018.00067/full

have your child taught by a fake teacher? What about a solicitor who has demonstrated their own corruption?[13]

So, digital communication facilitates both self-delusion and corruption. Anyone can lay claim to expertise based on sometimes spurious credentials. Indeed, the whole social media world depends on this 'affinity-inflation' in a way; since you are led to believe that you have some sort of higher affinity with your online community. When you are the company that you keep, it's easy to fool yourself that you know more than you do. The ability to express one's own genuine opinion is becoming reduced to sending animated emoticons rather than bothering to give any personal, nuanced, feedback. Not only is the opportunity to send a smiley face easy, but it also removes the potential for us to say the wrong thing, however this can mean we no longer feel or think very much at all past knowing we should send *something.*

Instant interactions have repercussions for the way we think. Instant interaction requires a different type of skill to the kind

---

[13] https://www.bbc.com/worklife/article/20190329-the-essay-mills-that-help-students-cheat

of critical and deep thinking that is needed to solve complex problems. It is possible that plenty of people can text or instant message all day as their means of communication and then master a difficult area of analysis but it is, in my view, unlikely. In order to become competent in terms of thinking and problem solving, it takes *real* experience and practice.

Then, there's our increasing compulsion to be multi-platform, multi-network, multi-media beings. The more browsers we have open at once the more productive, important and dynamic we feel. We are duped into thinking that someone with more tech is a 'better' person—someone financially successful, with lifestyle to go with it. Juggling lots of tech and simultaneously communicating with different people on different social media impresses us. Multi-tasking is the way that digi-tech suggests and even compels us to operate. However, it has been proved that genuine multi-tasking is not possible: your brain can only focus or concentrate effectively on one thing at a time—filtering out all the other 'noise', asking it to do more than this means that performance drops

Thinking skills and resourcefulness

across all the tasks we try to do simultaneously.[14]

Even the way that information is presented online can lead us to become distracted. Dozens of widgets, scrolling features and animations hamper our ability to focus on one element: we are bombarded with plenty of information but appear to internalise less and less of it. Important information is not clearly distinguished from the not so important (or commercial) and, in some cases, importance is based on popularity. Take the way many local new websites now work: news is now updated throughout the day not on the significance of the news but on its popularity. This means that genuine 'news' may be kicked out of priority slots in favour of popular local gossip and celebrity stories.

There is a tendency to drift towards information that makes us comfortable and, rather than searching for more information that might conflict with our values and beliefs, we stick with information and news that confirms our views. This confirmation-bias narrows down our understanding and contributes greatly to the increasing polarisation of opinions at

---

[14] https://hbr.org/2010/12/you-cant-multi-task-so-stop-tr

a global scale.

The level of concentration that we have is shrinking alongside these changes. A common joke is that the best place to write a secret is in a long book because no one will bother to read it. Already some young people believe that great classic literature of the past was actually created in the movie format. Many YouTube and other videos are creative and useful but new formats such as TikTok, although hugely popular, are often basically memes or 'lip-sync' videos; it would be a stretch to describe these as anything but marginally creative.

Humour is the bedrock of society. Wit is the mark of intellect and a pleasure to experience, whether you are delivering it or observing it. It saddens me that the online world is diluting wit to the level of memes. Sadly, the vocabulary of many people is shrinking to a level where they can't understand much of the word-based humour that kept people of the past alert and entertained. If you are uncertain of what I mean, watch an episode or two of 'The Two Ronnies' for brain-twisting comic genius.

Try watching an old movie from the 1950s or 60s and you'll see

Thinking skills and resourcefulness

how our ability to concentrate has already waned incredibly, the long dialogues and sophisticated plots require the ability to follow and pay attention that few of us now have. And they seem so *slow!* Contrast this with the hyper-paced, all-action movies of today and you'll see how the concentration abilities of a whole generation or entire society can change. It may be too early to tell exactly what the impact will be, but I am concerned. If you cannot concentrate when you are young, it makes sense that it will be hard to develop this hard-wired trait when you grow older.

Patience has, for some time been losing the popularity stakes, 'I need it done yesterday' attitudes have come into favour as indicating a go-getting, dynamic personality. I agree that you have to have a degree of inner urgency to drive yourself forward. However, the loss of patience that comes with expecting everything to be immediately broadcast or commented on is not about inner drive and motivation; it heralds the need for quick fixes rather than thought and investigation. Deeper consideration, although boring to a great many people, is what is needed to prevent costly mistakes in terms of decisions.

With this backdrop, how can we hope to develop the ability to be retrospective—to look back and reflect? As social incentives for deep-thinking are disappearing, social incentives for immediacy and more surface thinking are increasing. The challenge is to maintain the ability to hold the sustained attention that we need, not just to solve complex problems, but to maintain a sense of satisfaction with our lives. Constantly seeking the next immediate bit of positive feedback is bound to lead to disappointment.

Being able to think in a deep way; making the sorts of links that we need to solve complex problems, makes us resourceful. When we are given something to do with limited tools, human beings try and use cognitive ability to find solutions. As we become more and more dependent on digi-tech to do the hard work, where does that leave us? It is becoming commonplace for people to lack the skills for straightforward tasks like navigating somewhere in a car, working out a shopping list or making a plan without a pre-configured app of some kind. People now find it difficult to make any kind of appointment or social arrangement without the use of social media. Convenience is useful, but we do need

Thinking skills and resourcefulness

challenge to keep us motivated in life.

Within society, this raises the spectre of a very low level of individual and social resiliency. People have, in some cases, become pretty much functionally useless in terms of some tasks and depend entirely on technology. When something goes wrong people take on the persona of either a bear with a sore head or a demanding baby bird with its beak open. Very few of us will suggest a useful non-digital way forward any more for fear of looking old-fashioned. We are unlikely even to move to using a different tech solution. We have lost our ability to use our own initiative.

The capacity to consider something different is hampered by being actually or psychologically locked into using one app or another. This is why so many applications are free of charge to start with: companies know that once we get used to something it is very hard for us to change. Learned incompetence, fear and the misplaced loyalty of the herd mentality have the potential to leave us dependent on upgrading rather than using our own initiative.

This is bad, not just because we are pretty much screwed if the technology doesn't work, but also because people never get to find out that it is actually interesting and satisfying to do things for yourself, rather than have an app sort it out.

Social media can end up de-skilling us in a much more direct way: it can simply drown out some areas. The sheer weight of focus on the most popular topics, at the expense of the less popular, does that automatically. The skills and areas of resourcefulness associated with minority activities and specialised thinking then have the potential to rapidly decline. When people are encouraged to focus on a fairly limited range of interests and networks it is easy to see how the resourcefulness associated with some less trendy areas is quickly lost. In a homogenised world, diversity of thought is the loser.

Of course technology actually offers us a great deal of information and assistance to develop minority interests and knowledge and it is up to us to use this or not. The general move, however, is towards global trends and a loss of individuality.

Reaching for the tangible

The online world and gadgets are joined at the hip, each drives the consumption of the other, so I feel it is worth making some observations about the relationship between the two.

Gadgets are tactile. Because you can actually hold them in your hands or run your fingers along their silky edges, they have the ability to entice us in different ways to the apps that they host. Gadgets promise us enhancement and improvement over what went before. Most importantly, they mark us out as belonging to an exclusive network of followers and therefore reinforce our sense of identity.

Gadgets are an offline way of displaying your allegiance to the whole digital technology culture. If you walk around with the right kit, you are deemed to be 'better' than other people with lesser technology, an identity steered by references that you have picked up from your networks.

We all know *someone* hooked to their gadgets in a

questionable way. If your gadget appears dated then you may be familiar with the pitying looks of early adopters. The phenomenon of camping overnight and waiting around the block for the next phone has become commonplace. With each successive new launch the queues get longer and longer worldwide and purchases more and more frantic. This all adds to the cult appeal of the brand, conveying a sense of divinity about the whole 'latest release' drama. Once the hype is created it all becomes something of a self-fulfilling prophesy.

Most tech gadgets are overly complicated. Before purchase, we spend weeks comparing specifications and features that we won't use, even though some of us have literally no idea what the technical specifications mean. Once we have the item in our possession we start waiting for the next update. FOMO is a costly, but human, emotion. We fear being without our gadgets because of what they have become: an extension of ourselves and part of our identity.

The proliferation of voice assistants like Alexa is not seen as a worrying potential snoop-box able to tune into everything you say and making you dependent on it for things you could do perfectly well when you were a child; but an innocuous, playful and charming helper.

Tech Gadgets can be useful; however, the payoff is that they lead to a loss of understanding about how to do whatever they displace. This loss of skill is sometimes balanced by the gaining of new tech skills, so sometimes there is a trade off. Other times there is not. Take sat-navs. In many ways the use of sat-nav illustrates the issue of digi-tech altogether: the technology itself is useful, even life-saving, but people use it as a substitute for using their initiative and therefore are willingly de-skilling themselves. So what? Well being able to navigate non-digitally is a skill as old as humanity itself; should we lose it in a generation? We have reached the point where people are completely helpless when faced with just with a street map to navigate by. The intangible benefits of knowing where we are in a space extend far beyond not being late for a meeting. Some skills should be cherished.

There is a bit of a quiet revolution going on. Even as our love for hi-tech gadgets continues unabated, there is a parallel growth sector that plays to our human instincts and is much more conducive to preserving our skills: a gradual drift towards the old-fashioned, pre-digital (and earlier) and even archaic. This trend is happening in everything from products to services and is linked to notions of heritage, nostalgia, simplicity and quality.

For example, over the past few years, in response to the digitalisation of products such as books and music, a strange phenomenon has occurred: a return to the tangible.

Just as tech giants vie with each other to sell streaming music services, e-books, smart watches and even remove the need for tapping keys by the proliferation of digital assistants such as Alexa or Google Assistant, small businesses have reinvented tangible or lo-tech versions of goods which are now predominantly digital, as premium products. Whilst Spotify has charged ahead with on-demand streamed music, sales of vinyl, last mainstream in early 1980s, have skyrocketed. In 2019, more than $500million of vinyl records were sold in the United States, up 14 percent compared to 2018 and more than 20-fold compared to 2006 when the vinyl comeback began.[15] Although this is still only about 4% of total album sales it is a

---

[15] https://www.economist.com/graphic-detail/2019/10/18/the-strange-revival-of-vinyl-records

pretty phenomenal for a product that was considered all but dead and buried thirty years ago. Similarly, with the advent of e-books came the prediction that actual physical books would be no more. The expected demise of print books, to be led by millennials, never transpired. In fact, e-book sales have consistently dropped during the 2010s and now comprise only 20% of the market, with print books making up 80%. The reasons for this are manyfold and include pricing wars and legal issues, which subsequently have raised the price of e-books over time,[16] but one of the key issues is, obviously demand. Perhaps surprisingly, it is younger people who want to buy and read print books and older people who are sticking with their Kindles.

In an age of disposability a curious thing has happened: younger people want the real thing. This is not surprising, given the place of aesthetic appeal in the highly visual lives of the 'selfie generation': a digital download simply does not look as good as a real book or record. Considering the photogenic quality of carefully staged 'real' products, t is hardly surprising

---

[16] https://www.vox.com/culture/2019/12/23/20991659/ebook-amazon-kindle-ereader-department-of-justice-publishing-lawsuit-apple-ipad

that people are willing to pay more for the physical versions of books, photos, and movies. For the hipster generation these props are important.

One item that has all but been replaced by its intangible digital version is the photograph. Nowadays, many of us take thousands of photos every year, for some people it can be thousands per month. However, the vast majority of the photos remain forgotten somewhere on a drive, having never been looked at. Compare this with the 20th century, when photos were treasured and photo albums well thumbed and passed around on family occasions. The quantity of photos has increased beyond comprehension but alongside this the *value* has reduced. The perceived quality has shrunk with availability and disposability. It is interesting that, for the rare, very special occasions in life, such as weddings, we still turn to what we perceive to be the highest value format available: the printed photograph.

Quite apart from this, holding something in that is tangible increases the psychological sense of ownership an individual feels over the item. This matters especially when we subscribe to services (like Netflix or Spotify) when we don't even own a digital version of the product: we just access it from a server. The more we 'own' something the closer we feel to it and the more it matters to us and contributes to our identity.

The popularity of tangible products, especially high-end products is also important for another reason: real things, especially tactile objects that make a sensory impact, affect us at a psychological level. When these things are also associated with 'heritage' they take on even more meaning, creating a sense of emotional attachment and personal investment. This is the rationale behind the continued and growing popularity of luxury watch brands and clunky, old-fashioned electronica, for example.

The importance of the tangible is also evident in another way: the massive popularity of 'crafting' in the digital age. Making things is booming. From adult colouring books to traditional cobbling to building your own eco-house: hands on is definitely in. This makes sense. Actually 'doing things' permits the brain to do the things that technology takes away: making a physical effort, problem solving and approaching something one step at a time rather than multi-tasking. This old-fashioned 'slow' living is how our minds have traditionally worked and now, in these pressured times, we find a return to these basics, comforting and rewarding.

It seems the more traditional and tactile the activity, the better we feel. So, old-fashioned textile working, shoe-making and dry-stone walling are definitely desirable. Making mechanical things that work also satisfy our need to work out problems and even to fit widgets together—from Lego to motorbikes, fiddling about with stuff is really satisfying.

Digital technology has made life easier for a long time. We are now at a point when life is just a little *too* easy and our natural instinct for challenge is starting to leak out as boredom, frustration and a yearning to actually touch real objects and *do* something with our hands. As many people re-evaluate their priorities in life to make their personal wellbeing a bigger factor, the feel-good factor of the tangible and the hands-on will generate increasing numbers of followers.

Technology can compromise our thinking and behaviour. This can, ultimately, change the nature of society itself. I now want to focus on one of the key concerns about digi-tech and its

Reaching for the tangible

influence on society: that of the impact on communication and human interaction.

Digital Downsize

Communication and interaction

Digital technology provides us with ever more efficient ways to communicate with other people. We can now instantaneously connect with someone across the globe as easily as we can with someone in the next street. We can seek out people to communicate with in order to engineer our own tailored social network if we wish and so combat isolation and loneliness. With global labour movements, people living or studying a long way from home have electronic access to their families and friends on a screen twenty-four hours a day—you are never far from home with an internet connection.

For people whose ability to go out and about is restricted, for example, by disability or geographical isolation, digital communication offers an opportunity to develop relationships which, though not face-to-face, are important, meaningful and add enormously to their quality of life.

Social media communication offers us the opportunity to understand other cultures by communicating directly with people whose perspective we would otherwise have found difficult to access. In this way it has the power to increase tolerance and friendship. History is being created by movements made up of real people driving change with little more than a mobile phone and a twitter account. Quite aside from the politics involved, this is dramatically putting power into the hands of the people.

In learning and education and in the workplace, digital technology offers novel, interactive ways of communicating with participants able to share and modify ideas in dynamic ways (although the jury is out as to whether this always results in performance improvements).

For shy people, e-communication can mean a whole new world without the trauma of sounding or looking awkward. Messaging takes away the self-consciousness associated with meeting new people and can provide a buffer whilst we develop confidence. That's why it is such a hit with dating. On the other hand, as the internet becomes the main way in which people find love, so the number of dating scams has sky-rocketed. In the hope of companionship in an often lonely world, people seem more ready to trust. Unfortunately, whether through a dating scam or just a good old-fashioned email phishing, others are very willing to exploit this trust.

Digital technology can be a great tool in enabling us in to communicate together as the social animals that we are. Not only can we reach people virtually anywhere and at any time but we can also communicate with larger numbers of people than ever before. Whereas in the past we might have spoken to or phoned a few people by posting something online, we can now broadcast it to an audience of millions.

However, there is growing and increasingly public concern that the use of digital communications is damaging our ability to communicate, interact and socialise with others. The convenience and ubiquitous nature of e-communication means that we have to make a conscious effort to do something other than fire off a message. Technology has led people to write more and talk less. We message pretty much all the time and from anywhere. Nowhere is an e-communication free zone any more, unless artificial restrictions are in place. Unfortunately however, many places also now seem to be a *real* conversation free zone.

The rules of communicating have changed. For many people, shared personal experiences in the real world are no longer immune to the distracting call of a mobile phone screen. It used to be frowned upon when people out together did not exchange a word all evening, instead spending the entire time looking at their respective phones: now that has become routine. Many families don't eat together, preferring to grab more online time than talking to each other. A generation of parents is at risk of neglecting the need to communicate and interact with their kids, sadly preferring to spend more time on their phones than engaging with their offspring.

It is not just our immediate relationships that suffer as a result of our ever increasing use of digi-tech: we are less likely to be social to people in general. It might sound ironic that using 'social media' might actually make you less 'social' in real life, but it seems that this is the case. Because online relationships, to some degree, fulfill our need to feel connected to others, we don't see the point of doing things like helping our neighbours or local community in real life. Social media actually makes us less actually caring, whilst at the same time demanding that we portray ourselves as more concerned and involved, especially with online shows of involvement with the right causes: virtue signaling.

A digi-tech society is a voyeuristic society. I'm not just talking about exchanging messages and images. I'm also referring to the way that we search for distress online. The online world can be very mean and two-faced. Prank videos have been popular online since video-sharing began and have grown in popularity. At the same time they have grown more extreme in nature. Why do so many people apparently want to see others humiliated? Whatever the reasoning this, and the massive increase of cyber-bullying that social-media has spawned, are depressing and negative developments. Research now shows that most teens in the US, for example, have been victims of cyber-bullying[17] and sadly cyber-bullying may be contributing to the increase in youth suicides.[18]

The changes that we are experiencing because of the impact of digi-tech are completely unprecedented. Academics have

---

[17] Anderson, M. (2018, September 27). *A Majority of Teens Have Experienced Some Form of Cyberbullying*. Pew Research Center: Internet, Science & Tech

[18] https://www.cdc.gov/nchs/data/databriefs/db352-h.pdf

started to talk of 'evolutionary' changes (at least on a temporary basis) to the way that our brains work. The skills that gave people the edge in the past: face-to-face charisma and the ability to be articulate and persuasive *in person;* even just having a distinctive personality, may not be around much in the future. They may be replaced by the online skills of reaching as many people as possible, as quickly and as often as possible, over lots of different media. The content of our interactions will be different: shorter, snappier, and instantly replaceable by the next snippet.

In order to manage the tasks involved in checking social media and other apps, sometimes on a virtually constant basis, it appears that the neural circuits of our brains may be changing. As we are compelled to jump from one tab or app to another we are losing the ability to focus on one thing effectively; as Google provides easy access to all the information we will ever need, we are literally losing our memory. As the online world becomes more relevant in some ways than the 'real' world our brains also lose some of their 'social cognition' making us less able to relate to others offline.[19]

Our brains are not used to the speed of change that we are now undergoing. Researchers have shown that, whilst we initially may feel able to swing from one thing to another, shifting from tab to tab on our screens, whilst giving everything a bit of partial attention—this is not sustainable. This is because, contrary to popular opinion, we can't really 'multi-task'; we are just switching our attention very quickly. The brain still focuses on one thing at a time.

Initial feelings of self worth and competence are replaced by exhaustion when the brain can't cope with the overload of information anymore. Stress hormones such as cortisol and adrenaline are released into the body and chronic exposure to these can harm our mental and physical health.

E-communication may be fooling our brains into thinking that

---

[19] Firth, J., Torous, J., Stubbs, B., Firth, J. A., Steiner, G. Z., Smith, L., Alvarez-Jimenez, M., Gleeson, J., Vancampfort, D., Armitage, C. J., & Sarris, J. (2019). The "online brain": how the Internet may be changing our cognition. *World Psychiatry, 18*(2), 119–129.

we are having real, direct, biologically stimulating contact with people; this has the potential to leave us feeling misunderstood, hurt or cheated when things go wrong. Research has uncovered a significant boost in the 'trust' neurotransmitter oxytocin after just a short period of messaging; little wonder then that we feel good about bonding in this way and want this experience to be repeated again and again. We are fooling ourselves that using social media is the same as something more meaningful:

"Your brain interpreted tweeting as if you were directly interacting with people you cared about of had empathy for"[20]

In fact, this is just one small element of the illusion that digi-tech creates of us being in control of our behaviour when we use it. Far from being in control, our online, borderline inanimate lives don't satisfy our need for real autonomy and our brains begin to register that it is *us* who being controlled. That is when we either fall into line or react with frustration (compliance or defiance). Neither reaction is very healthy. Our minds need first hand experiences and signals from the

---

[20] Penenberg, Adam L. July 2010 "Social Networking Affects Brain Like Falling in Love." See: http://www.fastcompany.com/magazine/147/doctor-love.html

outside world to keep the neurons active and to boost the brains regeneration and health. That empty feeling many of us walk around with may be linked with spending too much time online and not enough in the real world.

E-communication has an impact on the way that we think. Communication is basically a manifestation of our thoughts. The way we express ourselves shows the world both our thoughts and our personality, digital communication has a profound influence on both. Much of the language used in messaging is basic—much more basic than allows for subtleties and a real understanding of deeper meaning. When a message is made up of abbreviations, slang and emoticons it limits what we can say. This has a knock-on effect when people are required to communicate in more complex ways and effectively reduces our ability to express our ideas clearly. With a restricted vocabulary our ability to think becomes restricted also.

Individual personality traits and emotions are not really definable when we communicate these aspects via smiley or sad faces or 'lols'. We characteristically fall in with what is acceptable in the herd; this might make us feel safe, but it does nothing to make us distinct in terms of having a unique personality. Then there is the bigger issue that we can't sometimes *see* the person we are talking to and *hear* their voice, we can only read the stumpy clips delivered to our screen. This matters, because the vast majority of meaning within communication comes not from the words but from other elements: our tone of voice, the expression on one's face, body language and so on. You can't really communicate the power of a period of silence or a look into someone's eyes in a tweet. Often the real *context* of what we are trying to say is lost.

Of course, we now increasingly use Zoom and other video-messaging to keep in touch. Some people like this and others don't. Although video messaging for work and education has been a Godsend during the Covid crisis, it lacks the genuine contact and nuances of face to face communication. It is these nuances that deliver better understanding and rapport.

Relying almost exclusively on digital communication (and for a growing number of people that is the reality) damages communication skills in practical ways. Our ability to

Communication and interaction

communicate using speech, away from the screen is reduced to the point that face-to-face communication makes us feel awkward. Real eye contact is a big factor. If you have ever watched a video on how to conduct yourself in a professional or personal situation the number one message is maintain (the right amount of) eye contact. This important element of communication is missing in (non-video) messaging. Even a simple phone call may become stressful: people can end up mumbling, or rambling on nervously. The further the method of communication is from real person to person contact, the greater the impact on our innate communication skills.

Face-to-face or even phone conversation requires a number of high level skills that writing messages on a screen does not entail. It requires an engagement with and an interest in the other person, rather than the impression that whoever you are talking to is waiting to move on to the next thing in a succession of tasks. Asking questions of other people, actively listening and being able to read other people's physical social cues, are also part of being a skilled conversationalist. For some people, these skills are being eroded by an over-reliance on screen communication and the consequent lack of experience of 'real' interaction.

Because e-communications are fast we expect instant responses to them. This brings a range of problems. If your instinct is to respond to a message immediately you are more likely to say something you regret—who hasn't been hurt by the curt response to the message we thought for hours about before sending? Misunderstandings lead to negative consequences from the unfortunate lost opportunity to, in extreme cases, death. There have been some pretty gruesome and shocking examples of where social media has played a part in murder, either as the catalyst, as a means to broadcast the crime or used to try and conceal the truth.[21]

I've already referred to the effect on attention span of being diminished in the digi-tech culture. A limited attention span affects not only the ability to stick to tasks for extended periods of time: it also affects the ability to communicate meaningfully. If you can't find the sustained interest and enthusiasm for a 'normal' conversation, you may find yourself

---

[21] https://www.crimeandinvestigation.co.uk/article/the-dark-side-of-social-media-deception-obsession-and-murder

Communication and interaction

dissatisfied and agitated. The ability to focus, and pay attention is fast disappearing.

Some now feel more comfortable looking at a screen than talking to others around them. This, to a growing number of people, is more interesting and enjoyable than 'joining in' around them. The brain, having been tricked by the stimuli of the online world, is fine-tuned to expect the immediacy, energy and relative certainty of life on-screen. If people increasingly use the option to conduct more of their communication online, they don't get the practice that is needed to communicate well in the offline world. This creates a vicious circle. The only way to improve face-to-face communication skills is by talking with people in real life situations. The more a person avoids interacting, the more afraid they are to speak to someone directly. It is a downward spiral.

In addition to the basic problems of participating in 'normal' conversations described above, high levels of e-communication, when coupled with low levels of face to face interaction may be causing a range of additional social skills problems. A healthy outcome of social interaction is a high level of self-awareness; we tend to learn about ourselves from the positive and negative experiences that we have, the knocks as well as the successes. This helps us make good decisions and communicate with other people in a genuine way. Social media turns this on its head: your identity is pretty much shaped by yourself, in the comfort of your like-minded community. You select how your identity is portrayed. Your profile is generally all about promoting yourself. Your focus becomes one of taking credit for positive outcomes and deflecting blame for negative outcomes.

When we take all feedback personally it has the opportunity to gain a significance that it doesn't merit and this can lead to problems. Online, a complete stranger can compliment us about something and we assume that they really like us on a personal level. Someone else can send a negative comment and we feel mortally wounded and vulnerable. We end up feeling confused and out of control.

The web, via social networking and e-communication, provides a breeding ground for narcissism and identity generation. The whole point becomes reinforcing one's identity, rather than

Communication and interaction

interacting with other people meaningfully and with tolerance. Identifying with causes (following trending worthy causes online) becomes a means of convincing others that you are a 'nice' person and boosting your popularity base. This 'virtue signaling' can sometimes morph into intolerance of others who disagree, even slightly, with the prevailing message. It seems that some people become hyper-passionately engaged with a 'cause', without questioning any alternative perspectives, to the extent that people who don't share the same views are hated. People hooked on protesting, seem lost without a cause to focus on and drift from one issue to another, often prompted by nothing more than the sound-bites shared online.

The online world provides both the 'evidence' for beliefs and causes and an easy and convenient platform to be dogmatic and insistent that people think like you do. People with very entrenched views feel that they can and must change the minds of others with equally deeply entrenched contrary views: this is very unlikely to happen.

Part of the problem is that the instantaneous 'friendships' and feedback systems that using social media, email and texting provide cause us to assume a level of closeness, even intimacy that is not really there. We are warned about the potential dangers online from predatory strangers but what about the people who are 'friends' but end up becoming pests you can't seem to get rid of? When it is insanely easy to add new people to your network, you make yourself vulnerable to misunderstandings at the very least. Fear of offending people makes us reluctant to remove even people we don't like from our networks.

Our social interactions online tend to become more and more polarised. This is not surprising as we are encouraged into simplifying our views about complex situations into 'like' or 'don't like'. We become accustomed to seeing both opinions and relationships in this black and white way. In the real world we may become unable to deal as well with ambiguity and uncertainty.

E-communication can also harm our ability to deal with conflict. Instead of addressing issues directly with someone in a mature way, we can just send a derogatory message. This

Communication and interaction

becomes the easy way out. When we use these methods to deal with personal issues it adds to the shallow, disposable nature of our relationships. We hide behind technology rather than confronting issues in a mature way. We are fast approaching a time when, for some, more personal ways of dealing with issues and the implied respect and legitimacy that that accompanies them, may become the exception to the norm of firing off brief, pre-configured social media messages or even just memes.

The frequency of contact and interaction may replace the quality of that interaction and even imply the quality and depth of relationships. We will feel that we 'matter' to people if we receive a lot of triggers and messages from them (even if they are automatically generated) rather than have conversations of any depth. The 'automatic alert' society lacks genuine concern or commitment and limits our ability to judge praise and criticism.

Communication and interaction

Impact on work

The nature of work and business is changing fundamentally. The changes that I have described in terms of behaviour and psychology must be taken into account in the workplace, especially since the move to hyper-digitisation post-Covid is inevitable. Otherwise we have a recipe for disaster: organisational frustration about why things aren't working in the way that has been anticipated, coupled with individual distress.

As digi-tech in our personal lives evolves at a pace that is sometimes hard to comprehend, organisations are under pressure to use more and more technology or risk being left out in the cold. Big players have the pressure of needing to be in the vanguard of progress and, of course, there is a significant lobby telling the business world that creating a hyper-digital workplace is of paramount importance.

This is a truly exciting and innovative time, both in terms of the technological tools and also in terms of the corporate and management behaviour that needs to evolve parallel to the use of these tools in business. Changes to the workplace, as a consequence of collaborative and social tools and the functionality of digital technology have been accelerated by the Covid-19 pandemic and bring new and exciting opportunities for business and organisations. New capabilities bring the prospect of staff connecting and coordinating more effectively but this needs proper assessment and management to avoid massive confusion and overload.

Skill sets for most jobs are now assumed to include e-communication and tech skills. Post-Covid, working online will be much more prevalent, if not the norm. Care is needed to ensure that the reality of working in the digitised, hyper-connected workplace does not leave the people aspect out of the equation. People are not, in themselves, digitised; we have natural differences in the way that we think and operate and consideration needs to be given to how the talents of people who want to work in a more offline way are integrated into the digitised workplace.

People need to be flexible and easily adaptable to fit well into the new work environment. Flexibility and adaptability are

Impact on work

positive traits, which should be enabled and considered premium skills. However other core traits long recognised and valued within human resources departments—traits such as reflection and in-depth analysis—should not be devalued as a result of this shift in priorities. Indeed, it could be the case in the future that people with 'face-to-face' skills and the ability to generate truly independent ideas (or even do things like write at length) will be at a premium. Creating a niche for people in this way is not the whole solution, in my view. We need to ensure that these skills are not lost from the workforce in general.

There are practical considerations to these new ways of working. People are working in an always-on, work-from-anywhere environment. The reality of 'telecommuting', a buzz word for a couple of decades, has finally arrived, thanks to Covid-19. Our devices provide us with the ability to work at any time; we just have to wait for the next cue to arrive. This has the potential to really mess up our work-life balance: even if your employer has a wellbeing-focused human resources policy, dedicated to ensuring your health and welfare—the *potential* to carry on working will still be there. The culture of our hyper-connected society steers us towards continually doing *something* online and for some people this will mean they feel obliged to work into their own time. Though this brings obvious business benefits, such as higher overall output, it also carries the risk of health and welfare problems.

Working remotely, although theoretically cost-effective, has downsides. It needs self discipline and self motivation to focus, to avoid distractions and to be productive. One way around this is to manage everything via constant messaging and interactive workflows—but is this best way to work, or will people feel increasingly pressured and stressed? Getting the balance right in the use of these tools is difficult. It can be easy to go too far and demand too much in the feedback loop. People report a need and preference to be together to prevent isolation; being at work involves far more than getting work done, the social payback for most of us of being with people and working towards a common goal is really important.

There is a bewildering array of tools available to enable employees to keep up with routine tasks automatically and at any time. Prompted by cues, employees can be guided through their daily work routines, theoretically leaving them free to concentrate on higher level tasks. However, my fear is that these higher level tasks never materialise, leaving people bored and dehumanized.

Technology holds out hope for the age old problem (especially for larger organisations) of working in silos. Interactive applications exist to support teamwork both across and between organisations. The ability to communicate, share knowledge and work on projects together online is undeniably useful; however, the added benefits of people working physically together, actually in the same room, need to be considered also.

Teamwork means more than sharing an online project folder. It may be difficult to keep abreast of what is an important issue or opportunity to collaborate and what is just 'noise' online. Just as with other factors in increasingly tech-dominated organisations, the outcomes are sometimes very different to the aspirations. I feel we need to take a step back before a new system is put into place to ensure that it is genuinely *better.*

The impact on interpersonal skills and relationships of people working remotely will be considerable. I've already talked about the way that conducting our lives online will, potentially, degrade our interpersonal skills. Work is one of the key areas where we practice and hone these skills. Already, we have the scenario where some people routinely send messages to people nearby, rather than actually speak to them. This trend has the potential to isolate individuals, create the misunderstandings that can arise when we don't have the non-verbal cues in a conversation and remove the potential for new ideas to be 'sparked' by face-to-face conversations. It is also not good for your health to sit in front of a computer all day. Although remote working will become much more usual in the future, it is as well to remind ourselves of some of the reasons why people have resisted remote working in the past: the social benefits of interacting with people in the office and the pitfalls of working long hours at home without the moderating influence a set time to physically leave a workplace.

As work becomes increasingly dependent upon people being hyper-connected, there are implications for fairness. Even

Impact on work

before someone joins an organisation the option to browse into their online identities is being increasingly used. Judgments can be made about people based on their pastimes, opinions and associations. Sometimes it may be useful to detect threats in this way, however I question whether this is a positive development. People have spent many decades trying to ensure that people are not discriminated against in employment; this has the potential to turn back the clock and actually add a limitless set of factors that people could be stereotyped about. Ironically, not having an online profile might be one thing that employers could look upon in a disapproving way. In addition, since you control what you say about yourself online, there are plenty of exaggerated and even totally untrue profiles out there. The need to fact from fiction comes into play.

The new connected culture that is being presented is one of a shift towards more flexible and collaborative ways of working, rather than 'command and control'. This works for highly motivated, competent and trustworthy teams and colleagues. The problem is that high levels of loyalty and motivation tend for many to go hand in hand with personal relationships and interaction at work, the very elements that might suffer if we are not careful. Away from environments where people are motivated enough to 'self-manage' online working, employers are likely to be disappointed by people trying to 'game' systems, especially if they already feel unfairly treated by changes in the wider economy.

Simultaneously, there is also an increased awareness amongst businesses of the perceived need to monitor their users and employees. With the risk that remote workers could be abusing the system, managers may need to employ a sophisticated array of checks and balances. Monitoring employees though IP address records, keyboard stroke counters, even web-cam surveillance, may become commonplace. Working with this level of scrutiny can lead to a high level of stress and a balance needs to be struck between identifying abuse and enabling worker autonomy.

At the lower-skilled end of work 'command and control' still rules—somewhat beefed up by the use of digi-tech. The use of scanners and sat-navs to guide warehouse and other workers is now commonplace, with routes worked out for maximum efficiency and each 'pick' monitored and timed. This way of

Impact on work

working potentially brings increased time pressure and stress at one end and the removal of context and autonomy at the other; although it must be said that some people really like working in this way as they feel it gives them a structure within which to meet personal targets. As always, when something becomes 'normal' it is accepted, so perhaps constant monitoring will be the future for all of us at work.

The impact of a changed work reality on power relationships at work also need to be considered. During the Covid-19 period front-line workers worked from 'work' whereas managers worked from home. This meant a 'virtual' disconnect between colleagues, either across the entire organisation, or between levels within an organisation. The impact of this disconnect on relationships should not be under-estimated and may have long-term implications of widening perceived status inequalities. It remains to be seen how power relationships will change after many remote workers proved themselves able to work effectively with a much reduced level of management.

Working remotely can bring greater autonomy and help people to find workarounds for aspects of work they previously disliked (such as the scourge of meetings). Productivity can improve, especially whilst home-working is a novelty situation. This should be balanced with the uncertainties and potential negative factors that remote working brings. Remote working may severely reduce the 'existence' of colleagues in the lives and minds of others in the organisation, leading to a breakdown in organisational culture and a rise in people 'free-styling' their own way of work, sometimes very successfully and questioning the need for management at all. In future, some managers may find themselves surplus to requirements.

Organisations will need to adapt to new realities. One example may be to cede power to people who have proved themselves in the remote-working environment. This can free up leaders to identify how to create organisational cultures with new ways of participating across the board, bringing together both remote and place-based working: a major challenge for the future. Post-Covid, leaders will need to lead a newly

Impact on work

empowered, perhaps anxious workforce during a turbulent phase of history: when jobs and sectors radically change and the spectre of new virus outbreaks persists.

Hyper-digitising the workplace is meant to make our work more enjoyable, run more smoothly and make us feel 'connected', aware and in control of what we are doing. With the tools at our disposal we can make things happen. Our work will feel more important and we will be influencing a lot more people. That is the theory.

It is true that we will be able to perform many more functions; indeed that will be required of us. We will also be monitored and give and receive feedback, potentially on a continuous basis. We'll be required to be available to colleagues and customers a lot more via the web. Although this might suit some people, already the problems of being overloaded and therefore overwhelmed are starting to emerge. In a hyper-connected workplace there may not be enough hours in the day to connect to everything with any real understanding. Furthermore, how do we assess what, out of the information backing up on our screens and in our inbox, to prioritise? In desperation, we might end up just guessing at what matters without knowing what we are actually doing. It is likely that managers will be just as pressured, so they might be of much help if people feel overwhelmed or confused.

In this context, losing touch with what you are doing has more serious repercussions than in the workplace of the past. Because things move at such a pace there is a danger that people respond to the most persistent tasks, rather than the most significant ones, or automate anything that can be automated out of desperation. In the hyper-connected workplace, if you mess up on something it is likely that many more people will be aware of it than in a more traditional setting. There are few places to hide and the digi-tech society rewards winners, not people who respond more to 'human' ways of working. At worst, given the weight of connected tasks, we could zone out altogether. Stress is a real and present danger to health and well-being in the digital workplace.

The ability of the brain to deal with the unprecedented amounts of information that we are now exposing ourselves to (not only at work but at home also) has only recently started to be studied. However, anecdotally it is clear that not everyone, not even some 'digital natives', can cope happily with the demands of the digital workplace. It is not just information overload that causes us stress, factors such as worry about the security of our data, our need for instantaneous validation and our constant connection with others, can all bring us down with a crash, or more likely wear us down until we mentally switch off.

Of course, when we are so dependent on being connected, that one of the key concerns is the reliability of the technology we use. Without it we are simply stuck. When technology malfunctions we exhibit all the frustrations that our primitive brains have evolved to display as part of the drive to discover solutions. The problem is that often we *can't find* solutions to technology problems ourselves, or even know how to fill the time usefully when a problem occurs—leaving us floundering around waiting for help rather than doing something constructive. Resourcefulness is diminished when we perceive everything to depend on online connection. Feeling helpless is not a positive outcome.

Trendy, hi-tech companies are naturally full of the kind of people that find juggling numerous hyper-connected, cross-platform, tasks relatively easy when compared to the rest of us. They are usually highly motivated, very well paid and immersed in environments that provide for enriched on and offline leisure activities as part of the workplace. Even here there can be problems for some individuals in dealing with the complexity and overload.

The transition to digital work will need to prove its worth in terms of outcomes. Concrete business improvements related to performance, profit, productivity and customer satisfaction will need to be delivered. It is possible, but far from certain, that the digital workplace, like the digital classroom will not deliver these improvements, or that improvements in some metrics are countered by reductions in others. Business should evaluate key areas upfront to ensure that the transition into a digital workplace is thought out from the perspective of people and outcomes before mistakes are made. Having a digital workplace can be great; getting it wrong can be a disaster both for individuals and for the organisation.

Impact on work

We are in a stage of transition where digital technology is being stuffed into the workplace without firstly properly working out the rationale or methodology to effectively choose, introduce or maintain the system. There is plenty of discontent, especially in sectors where the value of thinking and personal opinion really matters, such as higher education. Richards Hil's 'Whackademia' is a study of how universities have become workplaces where academics and other staff are compelled to use technology by way of virtual learning tools and administrative tools. The discontent shared by the anonymous contributors is palpable, as they describe technology to be a big contributor to a 'formulaic, googlised, dumbed down education'.[22] This study is from some years ago now but the concerns are still there; they have been joined by the loud voice of student discontent about enforced online learning as a result of the Covid-19 pandemic. The quality and experience of face-to-face learning is consistently felt to be better than online. There are fears (as in other sectors) that a two-tier system will emerge, with the privileged and higher-

---

[22] Richard Hil. *Wackademia: An Insider's Account of the Troubled University*. 2012 University of New South Wales Press.

paying accessing services delivered by people, whilst others have no choice than to access services online only.

This example of seething discontent and feelings of exploitation and betrayal amongst staff and customers (in this case lecturers and students) in just one sector may be indicative of more widespread feelings in the general workforce and community. Unless we begin to understand that technology is a tool rather than a goal in itself and recognise the potential for problems such as fragmentation and discontent, the introduction of the comprehensively digital workplace may bring a catalogue of problems.

Members of the public justifiably feel that they have a right to have direct access to some professionals, rather than access a service via technology. During the Covid-19 crisis, most GP surgeries in the UK took to liaising with patients online or by phone. This led many people feeling that GPs were shirking their responsibility to properly serve patients. Eventually the NHS reminded GPs that they needed to offer face-to-face appointments where necessary or face enforcement action. It seems that sectors planning to transition to mainly 'remote' services should be prepared for a public backlash.[23]

For those people with the responsibility of ensuring that a digital workplace is an asset rather than an expensive hindrance both to employee well-being and to business operations, there are some simple considerations to bear in mind.

Firstly, the rationale for adopting particular digital systems must be clear. Technology is a tool and like any other tool needs to serve a purpose, be this streamlining process and so increasing efficiency, reducing costs, increasing customer satisfaction through improving customer service, or increasing sales by marketing more effectively. It is foolhardy to buy into commercial technology solely because a salesperson promotes it as a 'must-have'. Be careful you are not just assuming that technology is the answer, because in isolation it is unlikely to be.

The digital workplace should be designed to be as easy to use as possible and it needs to make sense. Trying to

---

[23] https://www.bbc.co.uk/news/health-54138915

accommodate more and more interfaces and options often does nothing more than lead to confusion and the likelihood that people will end up making mistakes. The best way to get a design right is to conduct user research to see what people actually need and then undertake a pilot to show how any system is actually going to work in practice.

Careful thought needs to be given to the effect on employee well-being and work/life balance of remote working. Companies need to ensure that employees have time off from work tech and that the *expectation* to work relentlessly is not there. This is an essential consideration in the post-Covid world.

Collaborative tech tools should not mean that people *only* collaborate using digital technology. There are countless apps that claim to enable people to work more effectively by conducting meetings, projects and just about all communication remotely. Whilst there are definite advantages to bringing people together for work in this way (the most obvious is that it enables people to carry on working even if they cannot be together), remote working is no substitute for people actually getting together physically to work out

Impact on work

problems, chew the fat and get to know each other. By knowing our colleagues at a more personal level, in a less abstract way, we get to understand how we can each draw upon strengths, avoid offending or pressuring people and generally enjoy the process or working in a team more. Spaces and times need to be built in to enable people to be together person to person. Offline interaction should be encouraged.

Workplaces have had some success in implementing email free days and policies to encourage people to walk over to colleagues (before Covid). It might feel a bit weird at first if you are used to sitting and clicking, but talking face-to-face *does* strengthen our communicative abilities and it's what we need as a social animal. Work should enable people to shine and display their skills. The problem is that undue emphasis on digi-tech may allow some people to conceal their weaknesses and others to disregard areas of strength. Finding a way to highlight personal talents is more difficult when we are all hiding behind a screen.

Some employees may be compulsive users of digi-tech. Workplaces can propagate such behaviour, but they can also go some way to mitigating it too. Simple steps such as discouraging social media (unless part of the work role) and creating a culture where face-to-face interaction is valued and expected (organising new opportunities for people to meet in person if need be) be can go some way to balancing people's idea of what is 'normal'. Occupational health should provide lifestyle or medical advice and signposting at an early stage to help recovery and rehabilitation.

This brings me to the growing problem of digital technology 'addiction'—excessive, compulsive use of digi-tech. More specifically I'm referring to digital communications technology addiction which includes excessively surfing the internet, social media and gaming. This type of addiction could potentially become the most prevalent and damaging of the 21st century: especially dangerous because of the almost social desirability of being a 'tech-addict', the necessary and ubiquitous nature of digi-tech and the potential to affect people at a far younger age than other addictions. Internet

Impact on work

addition may not only affect work, it can destroy lives. In the next section I'll start to look at the nature of this phenomenon.

Digital Downsize

Compulsion and addiction

Many of us are now aware that the online world has its downsides. Over the past few years there has been a flurry of concern about the potential for internet addiction. It is easy to see why. Some uses of the internet: web surfing, gaming (and gambling) and social media communication, certainly have addictive potential. However, despite campaigns by concerned practitioners worldwide, 'internet addiction' is still not classified in the American Psychiatric Association's Diagnostic and Statistical Manual (DSM-5).

However, many people *do* feel that the internet is addictive and that awareness needs to be raised about the potential for people to become hooked. Even though it is not universally recognised as such, I'll refer to addiction and 'addicts' here, meaning people with a compulsion to use the internet or digital gaming to what would be recognised as a detrimental and excessive degree.

The human brain is constantly changed by our experiences. At some points in life such as in childhood and adolescence it is particularly receptive to change and 'imprints' made on the brain at this time are the most lasting. Our personality, feelings and behaviour—the things that make us 'us' are products of the workings of our brain. I've already described some of the behavioural change that digital technology has spawned around us: shorter attention spans, a reduction in interactive and social skills, memory problems and the inability for people to think in as abstract a way. These changes, when widespread, can change society.

We are now finding out that living a hyper-connected, always online lifestyle may also, for some people, result in addiction. There is always a scale along which any one person might find themselves in terms of dependency and its effects, but many, many people will now (sometimes even proudly) admit to compulsive use of the internet.

The severity of an addiction boils down to the extent to which it is affecting people's daily lives. We've probably all been in the company of someone who spends increasing amounts of time checking for messages and seems a lot more comfortable

Compulsion and addiction

when they are online than in 'real' life, when they may seem agitated and uneasy. To an addict, the rest of the world seems to grey out as they spend more and more time feeding their addiction. Even family and friends are neglected. When they are not connected, such people become restless and jittery. When called out about their behaviour they may become defensive or try, without success, to control their addiction, leaving them feeling guilty and anxious. Addicts will lie (including to themselves) about the extent of their problem. Aspects of physical health, such as sleep patterns and stress levels are affected—and it's probable therefore that the risk of health conditions associated with stress, such as cardiovascular disease will also be raised.

Of course, I am painting a picture of addiction as it affects someone with a potentially clinical health problem, rather than the majority of people who spend a little too long on social media now and then. We might not be addicts by definition, but we are increasingly aware that we are a society which is moving in that direction. The fact is that most of us feel considerable anxiety when we are without access to the internet and experience some pretty strong emotions when forced to be without this access for even very short periods of time (say a day or less).

The emotions elicited by being without an online tech 'fix' (or even being threatened with being without it)—being panicky, anxious, lonely, unable to cope— are so uniform that it is hard to ignore as a real problem and it may be only a matter of time before 'internet affective disorder' is included in the official list of psychiatric addictions. Some respected clinical providers, such as the Priory Group already recognise and treat internet addiction, offering self-help groups and counseling focused on abstinence and gradual reduction of internet use over time. Their rationale for providing these services includes the existence of growing global concerns about technology addiction, for example the Chinese government's decision to place restrictions on the opening hours of internet cafes and gaming after of several cardiac arrest deaths due to prolonged gaming in China.[24]

The conditions around us make it so much easier to fall victim to online addiction than any other type of compulsion. We are

---

[24] https://www.priorygroup.com/addiction-treatment/internet-addiction-treatment

Compulsion and addiction

connected everywhere, not just in our homes but on public transport, at workplaces, in social spaces—even in the 'middle of nowhere'. Worldwide, the race is on to connect the remotest places to fast broadband and 5G. Unlike illicit drug use not many people are going to brand you as socially undesirable because you happen to be online—in fact, the reverse is more likely to be the case.

It is far easier to give in to your desire to compulsively use the internet than it is for other addictive behaviours. Think about it: it is much cheaper to go online than it is to go and buy a bottle of booze (and zero effort); you are generally not going to be arrested for being online and being hooked is more likely to result in praise from your peers than being criticised. There are few sources of support available at present to help people who feel that they are already addicted, or becoming hooked on excessive use of the internet. Ironically, there is plenty of support from technology companies for people who want to use their products more.

Being online is socially desirable behaviour. Everyone we know is also online: gaming, surfing, messaging and so on. If we are not involved we are outside the loop of our friends and we risk, at the very least, 'missing out' on something and, at worst, being ostracised. When all of your social arrangements are made via social media what else can you do but join in? It feels good to be connected and we get the reassuring reinforcement of massages to our ego by way of validating cues (likes, followers etc) from our network. Being online is not just socially desirable, since Covid and the wholesale movement of access of everyday services online, it is now essential to function, in terms of paying bills, booking services and corresponding with service providers.

Feeling accomplishment and escapism in the digi-tech world gives us the dopamine hits that are so potentially addictive. Being able to be get though levels in a game, or win at online gambling, results in feelings of power and reward. For some, it creates a reality that is better than anything in the real world. Technology and social media companies use highly sophisticated methods to track our behaviour in order to encourage us to use their products more and more. We are *incentivised* to become dependent. Though tech companies may express concern that their products could lead to addiction for some people, they don't, really acknowledge the extent to which everyone may be becoming hooked to some degree and certainly show no sign of slowing down their efforts to enable us to use their products more and more.

Our gadgets deliver a constant flow of information that is always new and increasingly personal. We perceive ourselves as in control of what we see and do online. Online we think we can really be 'ourselves' more and people seem to understand us so much better than in the real world, which appears increasingly to be full of problems and dull in comparison. Just like anything else that makes us feel good: eating, sex or gambling for example, some people can become unhealthily dependent.

So what exactly is happening to our brain that makes us prone to becoming hooked? Well all of those little triggers and cues that are delivered to us: the beep of a notification, an alert or simply joining a game, lead to bursts of the neurotransmitter dopamine being released. Dopamine is at the heart of feelings of elation, it makes us seek things out and repeat actions again and again, whether it is drinking a glass of wine or going on a credit card spending spree. The effect of dopamine drowns out distractions to our activities, so that we can concentrate on our 'poison' without hearing the 'noise' around us. Over time we need more and more of the same 'hit' to get to the same feeling of euphoria.

Add to this our so-called 'hedonistic adaptation'—that is the fact that we are always searching for a better version of whatever we find pleasurable. We are always looking for novelty. The trouble is that it becomes harder and harder to reach the same level of pleasure that we first experienced. Eventually we don't really derive much pleasure at all, but we just can't stop anymore. We continue to crave for the thrill which our brain has associated with our digi-tech experiences but just end up needing more and more frequent 'hits', whilst deriving less satisfaction. Perhaps all of us, constantly checking our screens as we do, are somewhere on this trip already.

There is already a term for the fear of not having your phone around: 'nomophobia' which was coined during a 2008 study by the UK Post Office. The study found that nearly 53 percent of mobile phone users in Britain tend to be anxious when they "lose their mobile phone, run out of battery or credit, or have

Compulsion and addiction

no network coverage."[25] A much more recent study found that nearly nine out of ten students have nomophobia in the US and that it is associated with a range of sleep problems.[26]

Sleeping with your mobile next to you is the norm for more than two-thirds of us. Young people send thousands of messages a month and check for online messages every few minutes. Constantly checking for, or expecting, messages badly affects our concentration, producing a type of communal pseudo attention deficit disorder. This is compounded by the anxiety we feel when we are constantly waiting for something: many people feel a relentless pressure to keep up to date with trends and a sense of personal failure if they are out of step with these.

Constantly checking news-feeds and the like is a type of surveillance activity—triggered in part by habit and in part by

---

[25] https://www.royalmailgroup.com/en/press-centre/press-releases/post-office/lost-without-your-mobile-sounds-like-a-case-of-nomo-phobia/

[26] Peszka, J et al. (2020). 0180 Sleep, Sleepiness, and Sleep Hygiene Related to Nomophobia (No Mobile Phone Phobia). *Sleep*, *43*(Supplement_1), A71.

'fomo' (fear of missing out). Even more telling is our interest in other people's activity feeds, where we get to know what other people have been doing; this helps us to identify with others towards whom we have feelings of affinity. Unfortunately, we can thereby become drawn into an ego-serving or ego-destroying obsession. There are plenty of commercially shrewd, self-obsessed celebs around willing to encourage our interest.

For some, simply being online, browsing aimlessly becomes habitual. During work-time, the opportunity to use breaks to flick from one tab to another replaces actually talking to real people. Away from work, this behaviour can become magnified, to the extent that members of a single family are each absorbed in their own screens, rather than interacting with each other. For many people, especially the young, it can be hard to switch the screen off at the end of the day. When you can't control the amount of time you spend actively hooked to your screen it may have become an addiction.

Just as with other addictions, people will strongly defend their right to indulge, regardless of the fact that people close to them are concerned about their behaviour. For some people

Compulsion and addiction

this is compounded by lying about usage. Feeling despairing when your time online is cut short, is probably a sign that you are overly fixated.

Some people use their online lives not just to provide them with experiences that feel better than in the real world, but also in order to escape from problems in their lives, for example in their relationships or work. By focusing externally, you can avoid thinking or doing anything about things that matter in your life (and avoid the emotions that go with this). Being online becomes an addictive form of self-medication.

Feeling down if no-one comments on, likes or acknowledges what you post on social media is another sign that something is not right. If we are used to holding complex face to face interactions in the real world we learn how to deal with rejection and how to be balanced in criticising other people. In the artificial world of social media we don't have the opportunity to do this effectively. Without the emotional maturity we learn from in-depth face to face interaction, we end up unable to deal with differences of opinion, or even with silence, and take this as a personal criticism. Similarly, people 'unfollowing' or 'unfriending' can leave others feeling extremely rejected and depressed; if this is the case it could be time to think about whether we have a balanced view of the importance of online connections.

Of course, the online world offers the opportunity to compound any existing addictions too. Want to watch porn for hours on your mobile, gamble your salary away, or spend it all on shoes? It is all just a click or touch away and no-one need know.

The consequences of addiction leak into every area of life. Quite apart from the psychological hardship that being dependent on something brings, there can be damage to your overall lifestyle, physical health and relationships. People who heavily use tech are more prone to mental health problems such as depression and being sleep disordered. Even 'regular' users of digi-tech find it harder to sleep if they use technology late at night. The light from screens disrupts melatonin production needed to fall to sleep. What do some people do when they can't fall asleep? Go straight back online.[27]

---

[27] *John Cline Ph.D. Sleepless in America. September 2011.*

Compulsion and addiction

Sitting in front of a screen all day (or having it cradled in your hand) is not exactly going to lead you to peak physical fitness. The sedentary lifestyle, and the pale waxy look associated with the video-game addict, is no longer likely to be confined to gamers. Just as with any addiction, the more heavily addicted people are the more they are likely to neglect other essential areas of basic care such as nutrition and personal hygiene.

Given current trends, we will all need to become more tech-savvy to function. People might even feel that being obsessive use will give them an advantage at work. However, the subtle ways that over-use and over-dependence on digi-tech affect us take a silent toll. The nagging feeling that we are not *really* in control of what we are doing and the lack of genuine human interaction may leave us feeling rather hopeless and unfulfilled, or just worn out.

As far as family life goes, close relationships have the potential to be destroyed by tech addiction, as they do with any other type of addiction. Trust may be a major factor within some families where respective partners spend a great deal of time on social media, rather than with each other: cyber-widows and widowers already exist. For young people who have been brought up habituated to staring at their screens, the brain will, innately, crave more personal attention and problems may arise within relationships. There have been shocking cases in the media where children have been neglected and even died because parents have been too absorbed in the online world to care for them. This is an issue likely to multiply generationally.

Young people today are sophisticated digital natives. It is they who will shape the world as the parents, employers and citizens of the future. The next section will look briefly at the issue of young people and digi-tech: the 'digital-native' generation. How may the experiences of young people change the world as we know it?

Digi-tech and young people

When people speak of a possible impending epidemic of internet addiction, the examples that they turn to generally involve young people, the so-called digital native generations, who have lived their entire lives 'plugged into' the internet. The behaviour of young people and the short and long term effects of a truly from the cradle hyper-connected life are not yet understood, so one has to be careful not to speculate too much. People often surprise to the upside, so maybe we should be optimistic. Or perhaps we should be pessimistic? The future will be interesting!

Young people are influenced by what is happening around them, at home, with their friends and at school. The use of technology, for good or bad, is determined and validated by these influences. We would like to be confident that the technology, especially the communications technology, we introduce to young people is going to help, not harm them. Given the bias toward online learning brought about by Covid-

19 and the general trend towards online leisure, including the massive use to social media by young people, it may be that children and young people increasingly grow to depend on technology rather than see it as a tool to use within a life full of interesting challenges to be addressed using different approaches, both online and offline. Are we encouraging our kids to develop a range of psychological and physical health problems, or are those who are starting to raise concerns worrying too much? Since it is extremely difficult to undo problems that people develop when they are children later on in life, it makes sense to look into this now.

We now have a situation where the iPad is a useful way to pacify a grumpy toddler and where pre-school kids can pretty much organise their own leisure if given a device with an internet connection. Although convenient, this early start may not be doing kids any good. In fact studies have shown that too much screen time is implicated in a range of serious problems for young children. More screen time is linked to poorer progress on key developmental measures such as communication skills, problem solving and social interactions among young kids over time. These negative associations are independent of other factors that can influence developmental milestones, including parents' education, how physically active the children are and whether parents read to their children regularly.[28] Too much screen time is particularly damaging in the key period of age two to five years. For example, a study conducted as part of the Better Communication Research Programme by the UK government found that the number of children with speech difficulties increased 70 per cent in six years, blaming the rise on the use of screen-based gadgets as 'babysitters'.[29]

Is putting a computer in the hands of little Jack going to mean that he grows up not knowing how to socialise? Probably not. However, some children may have a predisposition to withdrawing socially, or other problems such as Attention Deficit Hyperactivity Disorder (ADHD). For these kids, the right human, rather than tech, contact is vitally important.

---

[28] Madigan, S. (2019, March 1). *Association Between Screen Time and Children's Performance on a Developmental Screening Test.* Child Development | JAMA Pediatrics | JAMA Network.

[29] *Department for Education. 2011.*

Digital Downsize

The pervasiveness of digital technology is a given, the question should be how to use it to benefit the growth and development of young people. Learning, for example, although potentially enhanced by online elements, is generally more effective when it is in-person. Motivation and enthusiasm for learning does increase for some kids when they use e-learning, but the jury is out as to whether these are the kids that might be highly motivated anyway. E-learning tends to widen attainment gaps between richer and poorer learners because it depends in part on the learner having a good environment in which to study, free of distractions and preferably with the support of guardians, both much less likely in less well-off households.[30] Although e-learning can be excellent and preferable to face –to-face learning for some young people, the evidence is simply not there to show that a digital learning approach, *in isolation* results in better outcomes. It is good and inspired teaching that makes a difference. There is even a risk that poor teaching might be hidden by the smokescreen of technology.

---

[30] https://schoolsweek.co.uk/the-cost-of-lockdown-attainment-gap-widens-by-up-to-52-for-primary-pupils/

Digi-tech and young people

The lives of young people at school and home are more integrated than ever before by technology. It is impossible to ignore the effects, positive or negative, of children's and young people's hyper-connected lives on their social and emotional development. Being hyper-connected means the potential for young people to discuss issues and get feedback from a lot more sources, especially from their peers. Ideally, this would mean that they question more and use their initiative to analyse and draw their own conclusions, having gathered and organised their thoughts. However, there is also the potential for the numerous stimuli (especially via social media) that occupy the minds of young people to exacerbate problems such as attention deficit disorder and a range of anxieties about appearance, uncertainty and attainment for example.

Distraction is a big problem. Teenagers are the greediest users of all types of e-communication, with the frequency of messaging being measured in the hundreds every day for some. When you are constantly waiting for the next instant message alert you are unlikely to be focused on learning. For younger children it has been suggested that close monitoring of digital technology use is a wise approach to militate against future problems. This might work at a very young age but, let's face it, young people have always been good at getting round restrictions. Will parents really be able to monitor usage when they themselves are probably playing catch up with the array of tasks they themselves are trying to do online?

What about physical health? At a time when obesity levels for young people are at unprecedented levels, enabling young people to spend leisure time online, rather than doing something physically active, is likely to make things worse. Apps aimed at increasing physical activity do not appear to have resulted in a significant improvement as yet, since the number of overweight and obsess youngsters continues to rise, despite these being around for some years now. Experts agree that digital technology used by kids in the evening also has a negative impact on sleep: just as with adults, the quality and amount of sleep declines. Being sleepy during the day is not a good backdrop for learning or working.

The greatest concerns in terms of the impact of technology on the lives of young people relates to mental health, social skills and behaviour. The popularity of viral videos, depicting anti-social behaviour or dangerous 'pranks' is a product of the lack of empathy that emerges when young people don't have frames of reference other than their own network, where they are in control and where their position in the hierarchy is set by sometimes chillingly sensationalist actions. Boundaries are pushed in order to get additional acceptance or credibility.

Even for the rest of us, encouraged by media invitations by to send in images for news and publicity, we now live in a period when, for some people, capturing an image comes before helping someone in distress.

The internet also facilitates and normalises expectations, particularly about appearance but also related to life in general. The 'selfie-generation' of millennials and those younger is marked by a focus on posing in pictures, with the expectation of praise and acknowledgment. It is rooted in the idea of hyper-'self-esteem'. Unfortunately, this self-centred focus may create a tendency towards narcissism and a range of body-image problems.[31] [32] Because it is hard to achieve your dreams even with a lot of hard work, when things don't go to

---

[31] https://www.csus.edu/faculty/m/fred.molitor/docs/selfies%20and%20narcissism.pdf
[32] https://www.irishtimes.com/business/technology/generation-selfie-exposes-itself-to-image-problems-1.3580917

plan extreme despair and disappointment can be hard to combat. Therefore, ironically, a focus on high-self esteem can easily flip into anger, extreme insecurity and even mental illness.

As a result of an obsession with the way that they look, teenagers, both girls and boys, are hyper-sensitive to image-related issues. Cosmetic surgery intended for adults (fillers, botox and the like) is now commonplace in the teen market. Unsurprisingly, eating disorders and body dismorphic mental health issues are on the rise in this age group. Another interesting but worrying phenomenon is the hyper-allegiance of young people to 'causes' and their reliance on this for a sense of self. Teens have always followed fads but the 24 hour a day, global nature of causes and fake news mean that followers now are susceptible to obsessive behaviour, exploitation and burnout.

Much more research is needed into the long-term effects of digi-tech on young minds so that parents and teachers (and society at large) can enable young people to grow into well-adjusted adults. It is hard to see how some young people will navigate this journey without succumbing to problems associated with an unrealistic sense of entitlement, insecurity related to their sense of self or just boredom and lack of challenge. Given the massive drift towards the homogenising—some might say 'dumbing down'—effect of online culture; it is hard to see how this can be avoided.

Crucially, we need to ensure that young people do not become addicted to the negative aspects of a technology that is part of the fabric of their lives. This will not be easy as, of course, the internet is a vital element of young people's lives: the ubiquity and essential nature of being digitally connected is unstoppable. Hyper online connectivity is like being connected to the national grid: without it you cannot access many aspects of modern life. By enabling people to connect and perform tasks at a speed and with a reach that was, until very recently, completely incomprehensible we place a great deal of opportunity into the hands of everybody, including young people. Perhaps because none of us understand the real repercussions of such a hyper-connected existence, we are currently living through a time when we are 'holding our breath' and hoping that everything will work out okay.

Then there is the worrying trend of social media being used to feed people's paranoid and dangerous predispositions. Social networking sites have been held partially responsible for a range of crimes including stalking and harassment, the grooming of young people by paedophiles, even murder. Even when we are told of the dangers of posting personal information online, many people still do it. Social media firms have clamped down on inappropriate content (especially that targeting young people), for example taking down sites that promote suicide or terrorism, or are likely to exacerbate mental health issues. However, removing these sites is a game of cat and mouse as new content springs up as soon as another is taken down. Young people often have confidence but they can also be naïve and even vulnerable. It will be one of the greatest challenges to ensure the online world does good rather than cause harm, especially in its persona as a seamless part of normal life.

The online world gives the unscrupulous the opportunity to win our trust. Our human nature has not evolved at the speed as technology; so we fall victim to scammers preying on our basic instincts of fear, love or to make money. I suggest that we need to take a more proactive approach to counter these threats. We can use common sense to tell us that we need to follow some very basic rules in key areas. For example, we need to think about the purpose behind the way we use digi-tech, whether in our personal lives or in a work context. More than anything else, we need to remember that online technology is a *tool* for us to use to enhance the quality of our lives. We should be realistic about what the quality of our lives is and not fall into the trap of assuming that we need to follow what everybody else is doing. We need to be willing to accept, without fear of standing against the status quo, that online technology could be harmful to us if we don't use it wisely. We need to be prepared to take a different path.

The next section, the concluding part of this short book, explores what you can do to use your online time more wisely as an individual

Digital Downsize

Wise decisions

OK, most of us are hooked into our online lives, but that doesn't necessarily mean that we are being harmed, or that we need to turn back the clock to life without digital technology. Digital technology is not a force for evil; indeed the services that it offers are often intrinsically pro-social. It is the choices that we make about its use that lead to the problems that I have outlined. These choices are, to a large degree, influenced by the way that digital technology, especially the online world, operates and is interpreted and popularised by society.

All of us are in living through one of the biggest changes in human history, a time when the very way that our mind works may very well change because of the impact of digital technology and, in particular, the shifting of so many aspects of life online. As societies and communities we are already seeing changes to our behaviour towards each other and our perceptions of what is 'normal'. It will be increasingly important to recognise that, as humans, we need to use technology in a manageable way, not let it manage and control us. Living online might be novel and enticing but it may not be good for us. We should be careful to retain 'human' activities and skills in order to fully develop as people and recognise the full spectrum of experiences that give our lives quality and interest.

For some people the use of some aspects of the online world, such as social media, has become very problematic. They may become drawn into negative or compulsive use. For people in this position, the process of re-balancing life so that technology is used healthily, rather than obsessively can be very challenging, made much harder by the fact that digi-tech is an essential component of virtually everyone's life.

For most people, digi-tech is a useful or essential tool for work, socialising and learning. It is when it actually affects people to the extent that it damages their ability to manage these basic areas of life that it becomes a serious problem. This is not necessarily related to the amount of *time* one spends online, especially as we all *have* to spend increasing amounts of time online in the course of normal life. It is when the quality and control aspects of life become damaged by the way that one uses digi-tech that it becomes a problem.

There is still some debate amongst mental health professionals as to whether use of digi-tech is an *addiction* or a compulsive disorder, in the same way that some people can't control the amount that they eat, for example. The field needs more scientific investigation. There are important questions to be answered about whether people who are extremely compelled to use some types of online tech (such as gaming or social-media) are also more likely to suffer from compulsive disorders anyway, or are more likely to be depressed or suffer from anxiety, for example. Common sense however, tells us that the explosion in the prevalence of mental health issues (especially for young people) in recent years is highly likely to be at least partly linked to the growth of the use of some types of technology, especially digital communications.

The good news is that for many people who feel that they may have a problem with compulsive or destructive use of online and other digital technology, behaviour change is possible using techniques such as cognitive-behavioural therapy or neuro-linguistic programming which enable people to understand what lies behind their personal excessive digi-tech use and change their behaviour in a planned and positive way.

People are recognising the need to change their behaviour in order to have more choice about the degree of control that the online world has over their lives. They feel that they would like to adjust the balance of their lives and make use of technology as a complementary, rather than controlling force in their lives. For increasing numbers, modifying the way that information and communications technology is used is an important factor in thinking more deeply about life in general.

By being aware of the pitfalls of using technology, both individually and as a society, we can implement changes that will result in us having a more balanced relationship with technology. Through this process we can make decisions that are likely to extend beyond our use of technology, to encompass how we want our lives to develop in general. Just as with any change it is not always an easy ride, but you don't have to go it alone and the results are worth it.

Changing your lifestyle

We do need to embrace the positive ways that our lives are being intrinsically transformed by digital technology. Even if we are unaware of it, virtually every process around us will be powered and controlled by increasingly sophisticated technology. The question is how to embrace this wholesale transformation of our planet, ensuring that we optimise the benefits of this digitised world rather than become victims of its dark side.

At a societal level it may seem hard for us, as individuals, to see how we can make a great deal of difference to what happens. Companies offer us services and the way that we use them, en masse, is up to us. Contributing to the online community is something that we choose to do; perhaps we want to be part of things for the greater good and accept a certain loss of privacy or even humanity as an opportunity cost of being involved.

Some applications of digital technology, such as social media, create such an impact that they change society itself. We are then caught 'in the herd'—a comfortable and safe place to be. We don't necessarily notice the problems until they start leaking into our lives and affecting society. I would contend that is where we are now at.

In such an environment, what can we do to balance the relationship between our online and offline lives? How can we, as individuals, implement steps that enable us to live in harmony with technology?

Awareness

Within many examples of our use of digital technology we have little option, or need, to question its importance. For example, in the delivery of public services such as health, we just expect technology to benefit us. However, in other areas we have the freedom to make our own decisions about the way that we use digital technology based upon the effects that we see it having on our lives. This applies particularly in our personal use of online communication and applications.

Once we are aware of the potential pitfalls we can make

Changing your lifestyle

conscious decisions, using information to decide what we want to do. Once we *understand* how our use of digital technology networks has an impact both on us as individuals and on the hyper-connected society that we live in, we can choose whether to modify our behaviour.

For example, it comes as a surprise to some people that they, themselves, actually comprise the framework that social media and other digital technology relies upon. Rather than technology becoming a tool for us, we have become a tool for technology—in this case providing the internet with its life-blood: content.

Greater awareness means that we create choices about what we participate in. With awareness comes a degree of control in terms of decisions. For example, we may choose to take additional steps to protect ourselves and our information, not only by instituting security measures online but also by reserving some of our true selves for the real world.

Balance

In an 'always on' world we need to appreciate that we can

switch off for a while. Whilst we interface with the digi-tech world via devices (rather than them being implanted physically into us, which many believe will happen in the not too distant future) we have the option to restrict the time that we spend 'connected'. When you are used to being hyper-connected, switching off is not easy at first—a concentrated effort is required. The biggest challenge for many people is the feeling that you might 'miss out' on something if you are not watching your Facebook, Instagram or Twitter account eighteen hours a day—FOMO.

For many people switching off social media totally is unwelcome, scary and unnecessary. Just laying aside a part of every day when you switch off your gadgets, or leave them behind for a time, makes a big difference to one's ability to cope without feeling compelled to constantly check a screen. Pretty soon you'll realise that you are not missing out on that much and may even feel that you want to integrate more tech-free time into your life. Having access to something all the time makes us lazy, in that we take it for granted that it will be there whenever we want it. Taking time away from digi-tech means that we are more likely to appreciate the value of it when we use it. Rather than being a rather mindless activity, it becomes something that we actually consider and appreciate.

By making time for other activities that don't depend on the internet we increase our resourcefulness and probably make some *real* friends along the way. When we slim down what we do online we start to use time in a more conscious way. When we decide to do other things with our time, rather than sit in front of a screen, we can investigate what it is that we really like doing. Rather than messaging for the sake of it we will actually have something to say.

Slim down

Although it may make you look impressive, constantly switching from one online task to another is not really that smart. Often, this leads to 'burn-out' and the inability to focus on one thing. Of course, some of the pressure to 'multi-task' may come from external sources such as work, but we put a lot of the load willingly on ourselves, either because we feel we actually *need* to be doing lots of different things all the time, or because we assume this makes us more competent in the eyes of other people. More often than not, neither of these is the case.

Multiple social-media accounts (to avoid 'missing' anyone) are unmanageable. Using automated posting is strategic but sometimes confusing. Using countless apps is stressful and involves an ever steepening learning curve. To take back control I suggest that we sit back and really assess what it is that we use online and then see where the excess baggage is. If you can't really manage without the layers, fair enough. For most people though it is remarkable just how much repetition there is in how we use our online time.

It is good to share but not when it becomes more important than enjoying an experience, or when the photo opportunity is more important than the actual moment in time. If you can absorb yourself in something and enjoy it without needing to tweet, Instagram, Facebook or otherwise send it over the airwaves the second you do it, then you've probably found something that you truly enjoy, rather than simply want to display to other people. Of course there are things that you want to share with your friends and family, or with people with the same interests as you, but the habit of posting absolutely everything to absolutely everyone devalues everything that you send.

Switch off the noise

Much of our digi-tech use is essentially noise: the 24/7 streaming of news, activity feeds and commercial hype. We don't really listen to it and yet we are strangely hypnotised and compelled to watch it again and again as it rolls on. Think about whether you *really* want to watch the same thing five times in a day. Is it really likely to change? It is more likely that you are just filling space? Is it worth feeling tired and overwhelmed just to stare at the same thing over and over again?

All the time that you are trapped in this rinse and repeat culture, you are preventing the possibility of using the time in another (more fulfilling) way. Could it be that you fear doing something different and your brain is manufacturing the perfect excuse of being busy 'doing something'?

Then there is the 'noise' of all the pleasing signs of validation: the pings and bleeps of messages and alerts. Of course it is not 'just' noise. In common with the screen ident or the jingle for the next rolling news-feed, these markers provide positive reinforcement—a mark of familiarity that we respond to by needing more and more.

It is harder to steer away from engaging with messages than watching content of course, because they are something special—something that we see as confirming that we are special enough to be contacted personally. Whilst deleting your social media accounts is the most definitive way of getting away from these particular dopamine surges, this is not acceptable (or desirable) for most people. Having the willpower to resist checking your device every few minutes is not easy but, once achieved, is likely to herald a sense of freedom from being compelled to live constantly watching for new messages.

Concentrate

Whatever we do of any significance deserves our full attention, free from the distractions that digital technology offers us. Most of us know what it feels like to settle down to do a piece of work, or revise for an exam and then spend a significant proportion of the time we allocate ourselves looking for a distraction, be it settling down for yet another coffee or leafing through online junk. Conveniently, digital distractions are automated and even legitimised, for example when the 'new message' notification pops up on-screen.

Once we have removed the distractions—and that means turning off the automatic notifications and putting our gadgets out of sight and reach whilst we are doing something else—we then need to retrain ourselves to give our *full* awareness to our tasks.

Distraction means that people often don't make progress with the task at hand. In addition, you may have to return again and again to finish a task; leaving you feeling drained and frustrated; something that most of us will confirm from our own experience. By recognising a digital intrusion and pulling yourself back to whatever you were originally focused on, you can learn how to avoid this threat to your personal productivity. The Rudolf Steiner concentration exercise—clearing the mind of all superfluous 'will-o'-the-wisps' of thought in order to sharpen the focus on one thing—can be an effective way to regain focus.[33]

Once you actively start to concentrate more you may notice that your ability to enjoy life in general also improves. It is not uncommon for people to start to notice small things around them for the first time, to find their attention span growing and for them to actually become interested in life. It sounds clichéd, but it is amazing what you start to see when you actually open your eyes to real experiences.

Think and Relax

We seem to have forgotten how to think and relax. Our brains need to do both. By thinking I mean deep concentration as well as letting your mind wander and develop ideas. Being constantly 'wired' into the many different stimuli and tasks of a tech-dominated world doesn't allow our mind to do this. I suggest that we 'unplug' and practice using our ancient cognitive skills as part of a routine, using both convergent (focused) thinking and divergent (unfocused 'creative')

---

[33] https://www.rudolfsteiner.org/fileadmin/user_upload/gs-letters-asa/Subsidiary_Exercises_RS.pdf

thinking. Although thinking without the influence of technology may initially feel completely alien, this is what we our brains are designed to do. By thinking deeply we are saying to ourselves that our own thoughts are important enough to be the priority, rather than our gadgets and applications. This builds our self-esteem.

We also need time away from processing information. We need to relax to keep body and mind together. By relaxing I mean emptying our minds of niggling bits of noise and distractions. I'm not suggesting that everyone turns to meditation or yoga, but I do suggest reducing the noise and setting aside time away from technology in which to unwind. For some people finding simple activities that help them recharge, things like walking, really help.

Use your potential

Once we free ourselves from being slaves to digital communications we can start thinking about how technology can work for us. Rather than automatically putting technology on a pedestal, we should think about the basics first: what is it that I want technology to do for me; how can it improve upon what is already happening; what are the criteria I need it to fulfil before I adopt it and how am I going to use it so that it benefits rather than disadvantages me. This attitude and process will help people to avoid blindly following the latest tech thing, whether for leisure or work.

There are some areas of our lives that are sacrosanct, something we should become acutely aware of. In particular this means our face to face interaction with other people and our ability to think and act in real life. We need to become more aware of the potential of our use of digital technology to disrupt our skills. Alongside this we should take active steps to preserve these skills, both in our personal life and at work. This won't be easy, given the massive weight and reach of technology that we are overwhelmed by nowadays. However, we can make conscious efforts to make the time and undertake the activities that enable us to use and practice skills such as deep thinking, face-to-face interaction and using our ingenuity in 'low-tech' environments. I suggest that these skills are encouraged from an early age.

When digital technology enables us to extend and further

develop skills we should use it for this purpose. The online world confers access to a diversity of people and new experiences, we can use this to think more broadly and take action to extend ourselves. The online world and technology in general has tremendous potential to inspire us. We need be active in using technology to expand life, not diminish it.

By developing our offline 'real' personality and non-techified skills we end up feeling and being more productive. Once we have eliminated the constant whirr from the background we can focus on what we really need to attend to in order to make life more fulfilling.

Use digital technology smartly

Using digital technology doesn't have to detract from your life. For example, if you are selective about the way that you use social media it can become a tool that complements the rest of your life, rather than holding you in its grip. The aim of having a social media network should be to add the potential for quality interactions, not to have as large a follower base as possible. Valuing yourself by the size of your network is an illusory and easily broken type of self-esteem. Simply pruning down your network is likely to make you think about why some people were there in the first place.

When you use social media, your brain will thank you for using it imaginatively. Creating something original and interesting, rather than just re-tweeting something or sending a smiley face, is likely to feel more fulfilling. The feedback you get should also lead to greater payback for your interactive skills. If you can combine what you do online in an engaging way with your offline life, then you've pretty much ticked all the boxes for healthy and interesting use of this aspect of digital technology.

It is smart to use tech as a tool to give you more time to actually do things that you enjoy. If you hate shopping, ordering groceries online might free you up to do something that is more meaningful; filling the time with sitting and scrolling through click-bait may not be such a good use of your new found time. Sometimes, giving something a bit of a rest can make us see it in a new way. This may be true of using online tech.

Changing your lifestyle

It goes without saying that I wouldn't recommend using your time online to satisfy your other vices or transferring online addictions like gambling from the online to the offline world.

Changing your lifestyle

STEP-BY-STEP

Making a decision to re-balance your life is good. Actually changing can be hard. Here are some bullet points to help:

Cold turkey
Switching off completely, for a limited time of a few days or more, will probably be excruciating but it may also bring an acute level of awareness about the time that we spend 'locked-in', how we use tech in the wrong way or ignore other parts of our lives. If you can only access essential services online, you will need to arrange for someone else to access these for the duration.

Increase your digi-tech free time
If you are used to being 'always on' going, try gradually introducing tech-free times. If you are used to accessing social media eighteen hours a day, cut this down to seventeen hours

to start with and then reduce by an hour or so every couple of days. Use your 'new time to enrich your life. Gradually decrease your online time to a level where it does not dominate.

Keep one foot in the tangible world

When you have an online and offline way to do the same thing (read a book, for example) vary the format so that you keep one foot in the 'tangible' world. Spend some time every day doing something that is 'hands-on' from climbing a hill to painting a picture. Take up a craft or hands-on trade.

Don't follow the click-bait

It is easy to follow from one link to the next to the next. Before you know it hours have disappeared and you have flicked through hundreds of pics of celebrities you don't even recognise. Stop. Keep browsing to a set maximum in terms of layers and keep your focus on your original task.

Changing your lifestyle

Break the 24 hour habit

Virtually all of us all check our screens first thing in the morning and last thing at night. Allow a maximum amount of time for morning and evening scrolling. In fact, spend the last hour or two before sleep tech free. By giving your brain some breathing space you'll sleep better and start the day in control.

Learn how to live

Activities such as meeting with friends and family, enjoying the outdoors and looking around us are now things we do with the aim being post the images on social media. Doing these activities *without* posting is an alien concept. Start to experience life away from digital imprisonment by doing things you value without broadcasting them.

Get support

It is easier to make changes to life with the support of friends, family or a support group. Tell people if you need help limiting negative tech-times so that they can help you stay on track. You should seek professional medical assistance if you are clinically unwell as a result of your lifestyle.

Get new skills

Learn through experience how to use the skills that digi-tech may have compromised: thinking, interaction, solving problems and enjoying activities together with other people. Practice these skills and pass them on to others.

THE NEW YOU

If you think that your life might be improved by 'downsizing' the digital in your life you've taken an important first step to changing things for the better: you've appreciated that things *need* to change. However, this is only the first step. Most meaningful change is not easy and the more entrenched your existing (albeit understandable and unwitting) dependence on technology, the more of a challenge it could be.

You need *willpower* to change your behaviour. For instance, since social media works by eroding away your willpower and enticing you into following its controls and suggestions, it might be quite a challenge sticking to the plan for some people. This is where you need to gather your resources, be

Changing your lifestyle

they friends, a personal goal and reward plan or a support service.

Alongside this, you also need to manage your own and other people's expectations, so that you are not setting yourself up to fail. You also need to be aware of where to invest your energies and be prepared for a bit of 'collateral damage' by way of some people's reactions. In other words, you might lose a few 'friends' along the way.

It is likely that most people around you will be up to their eyeballs in digi-tech without thinking about how they are using it. Engineering and articulating your decision to downsize your tech use might not make sense to your friends at first. Moving forward may involve creating distance from some of your previous networks, whilst you gather inner strength and support. Real friends, by definition, support our development as people, so they will be there to share your journey. Adjusting one's lifestyle is not an instant thing—you don't just go to bed one day and wake up the next day as a different person. It could several months (or longer) to adjust to new routines and ways of thinking.

The aim will be different for different people, for some it could be a comprehensive 'unplugging'. For these people, living a life with minimal use of digital technology, with technology taking a backseat, is the goal. For most people, the goal will not be shunning digi-tech but re-positioning it as a tool to use in an informed and creative way to enhance, rather than dominate life. By being proactive, people can 'reclaim' digi-tech to use in a healthy and balanced lifestyle. Nothing will slow down the relentless development of digital technology and communications. However, by being aware of its value within the context of our 'real' lives the aim is to change our relationship with technology so that we expect it to meet the needs of our higher-level aspirations. We have a responsibility to reject ways of using it that steer us towards banality and frustration.

The process to implement the awareness and learn the skills needed to change the balance between technology and human-centredness is different for everyone. Some people will struggle, whilst others will enjoy new-found freedom and self-awareness from the beginning.

Changing your lifestyle

By downsizing the control of digi-tech over your life you can develop a lifestyle where technology contributes to health, happiness and well-being. I hope that I've inspired you to start this process.

Digital Downsize

ABOUT THE AUTHOR

Nyla Naseer lives in Birmingham, United Kingdom. She is a writer and social commentator.

A career that spans working in warehouses to boardrooms has enabled her to experience how organisations operate and the judgments they make. This has prompted an exploration of why people and societies behave as they do.

The dominant themes of Nyla's writing are: the innate need of people to be 'human' in both positive and negative ways, the stories that emerge from the soup of change, and the need to understand how we become influenced by others. She writes both non-fiction and fiction exploring these themes. Her works of fiction are mainly about the adventures of contemporary outsiders.

Her non-fiction writing is centred on the tensions between social change and 'human-ness'. Nyla's interest in technology spans legal, economic and technical issues but is most keenly devoted to the impact on individual and social relations. She is a life-long advocate of simplicity, walking and nature and writes about the necessity to revive these elements as part of a human-centred life.

Nyla has a BSc in Management Science, a Master of Science degree in Urban Regeneration and a Master of Law degree. She is also a PGCE qualified trainer, a qualified personal fitness trainer and a certified NLP practitioner.

Away from her writing she can frequently be seen pounding

the paths as a long-distance hiker.

www.ingramcontent.com/pod-product-compliance
Lightning Source LLC
Chambersburg PA
CBHW020255030426
42336CB00010B/770